James Thomas Fields

Old Acquaintance. Barry Cornwall and Some of His Friends

James Thomas Fields

Old Acquaintance. Barry Cornwall and Some of His Friends

ISBN/EAN: 9783337020248

Printed in Europe, USA, Canada, Australia, Japan

Cover: Foto ©ninafisch / pixelio.de

More available books at **www.hansebooks.com**

Copyright, 1876, by
JAMES T. FIELDS.

University Press: Welch, Bigelow, & Co.,
Cambridge.

To the Wife of BRYAN WALLER PROCTER, and the Mother of ADELAIDE ANNE PROCTER, these Recollections are cordially inscribed.

"Old Acquaintance, shall the nights
　　You and I once talked together,
Be forgot like common things?"

"His thoughts half hid in golden dreams,
Which make thrice fair the songs and streams
　　Of Air and Earth."

"Song should breathe of scents and flowers;
　　Song should like a river flow;
Song should bring back scenes and hours
　　That we loved,—ah, long ago!"

BARRY CORNWALL.

These pages are reprinted (with some additions) from "Harper's Magazine," where they first appeared a few months ago.

April, 1876.

"BARRY CORNWALL"

AND SOME OF HIS FRIENDS.

 FIRST saw the poet five-and-twenty years ago, in his own house in London, at No. 13 Upper Harley Street, Cavendish Square. He was then declining into the vale of years, but his mind was still vigorous and young. My letter of introduction to him was written by Charles Sumner, and it proved sufficient for the beginning of a friendship which existed through a quarter of a century. My last interview with him occurred in 1869. I found him then quite feeble, but full of his old kindness and geniality. His speech was somewhat difficult to follow, for he had been slightly paralyzed not long before; but after listening to him for half an hour it was easy to understand nearly every word he uttered. He spoke with warm feeling of Longfellow, who had been in London during that season, and had called to see his venerable friend before proceeding to the Continent.

"Was n't it good of him," said the old man, in his tremulous voice, "to think of *me* before he had been in town twenty-four hours?" He also spoke of his dear companion, John Kenyon, at whose house we had often met in years past, and he called to mind a breakfast party there, saying, with deep feeling, "And you and I are the only ones now alive of all who came together that happy morning!"

A few months ago,* at the great age of eighty-seven, Bryan Waller Procter, familiarly and honorably known in English literature for sixty years past as "Barry Cornwall," calmly "fell on sleep." The schoolmate of Lord Byron and Sir Robert Peel at Harrow, the friend and companion of Keats, Lamb, Shelley, Coleridge, Landor, Hunt, Talfourd, and Rogers, the man to whom Thackeray "affectionately dedicated" his "Vanity Fair," one of the kindest souls that ever gladdened earth, has now joined the great majority of England's hallowed sons of song. No poet ever left behind him more fragrant memories, and he will always be thought of as one whom his contemporaries loved and honored. No harsh word will ever be spoken by those who have known him of the author of "Marcian Colonna," "Mirandola," "The Broken Heart," and those charming lyrics which rank the

* October, 1874.

poet among the first of his class. His songs will be sung so long as music wedded to beautiful poetry is a requisition anywhere. His verses have gone into the Book of Fame, and such pieces as "Touch us gently, Time," "Send down thy winged Angel, God," "King Death," "The Sea," and "Belshazzar is King," will long keep his memory green. Who that ever came habitually into his presence can forget the tones of his voice, the tenderness in his gray retrospective eyes, or the touch of his sympathetic hand laid on the shoulder of a friend! The elements were indeed so kindly mixed in him that no bitterness or rancor or jealousy had part or lot in his composition. No distinguished person was ever more ready to help forward the rising and as yet nameless literary man or woman who asked his counsel and warm-hearted suffrage. His mere presence was sunshine to a new-comer into the world of letters and criticism, for he was always quick to encourage, and slow to disparage anybody. Indeed, to be *human* only entitled any one who came near him to receive the gracious bounty of his goodness and courtesy. He made it the happiness of his life never to miss, whenever opportunity occurred, the chance of conferring pleasure and gladness on those who needed kind words and substantial aid.

His equals in literature venerated and loved him. Dickens and Thackeray never ceased to regard him with the deepest feeling, and such men as Browning and Tennyson and Carlyle and Forster rallied about him to the last. He was the delight of all those interesting men and women who habitually gathered around Rogers's famous table in the olden time, for his manner had in it all the courtesy of genius, without any of that chance asperity so common in some literary circles. The shyness of a scholar brooded continually over him and made him reticent, but he was never silent from ill-humor. His was that true modesty so excellent in ability, and so rare in celebrities petted for a long time in society. His was also that happy alchemy of mind which transmutes disagreeable things into golden and ruby colors like the dawn. His temperament was the exact reverse of Fuseli's, who complained that "*nature* put him out." A beautiful spirit has indeed passed away, and the name of " Barry Cornwall," beloved in both hemispheres, is now sanctified afresh by the seal of eternity so recently stamped upon it.

It was indeed a privilege for a young American, on his first travels abroad, to have "Barry Cornwall" for his host in London. As I recall the memorable days and nights of that long-ago period, I wonder at the good fortune which brought me into such relations with him, and I linger with profound gratitude over his many acts of unmerited kindness. One of the most intimate rambles I ever took with him was in 1851, when we started one morning from a book-shop in Piccadilly, where we met accidentally. I had been in London only a couple of days, and had not yet called upon him for lack of time. Several years had elapsed since we had met, but he began to talk as if we had parted only a few hours before. At first I thought his mind was impaired by age, and that he had forgotten how long it was since we had spoken together. I imagined it possible that he mistook me for some one else; but very soon I found that his memory was not at fault, for in a few minutes he began to question me about old friends in America, and to ask for information concerning the probable sea-sick horrors of an Atlantic voyage. "I suppose," said he, "knowing your infirmity, you found it hard work to stand on your immaterial legs, as Hood used to call Lamb's quivering limbs." Sauntering out into the street, he went on in a quaintly humorous way to imagine what a rough voyage must be to a real sufferer, and thus walking gayly along, we came into Leadenhall Street. There he pointed out the office where his old friend and fellow-magazinist, "Elia," spent so many years of hard work from ten until four o'clock of every day. Being in a mood for reminiscence, he described the Wednesday evenings he used to spend with "Charles and Mary" and their friends around the old "mahogany-tree" in Russell Street. I remember he tried to give me an idea of how Lamb looked and dressed, and how he stood bending forward to welcome his guests as they arrived in his humble lodgings. Procter thought nothing unimportant that might serve in any way to illustrate character, and so he seemed to wish that I might get an exact idea of the charming person both of us prized so ardently and he had known so intimately. Speaking of Lamb's habits, he said he had never known his friend to drink immoderately except upon one occasion, and he observed that "Elia," like Dickens, was a small and delicate eater. With faltering voice he told me of Lamb's "givings away" to needy, impoverished friends whose necessities were yet greater than his own. His secret charities were constant and unfailing, and no one ever suffered hunger when he was by. He could not endure to see a fellow-creature in want if he had the means to feed him. Thinking, from a depression of spirits which Procter in his young manhood was once laboring under, that perhaps he was in want of money, Lamb looked him earnestly in the face as they were walking one day in the country together, and blurted out, in his stammering way, "My dear boy, I have a hundred-pound note in my desk that I really don't know what to do with: oblige me by taking it and getting the confounded thing out of my keeping." "I was in no need of money,"

COLERIDGE.

said Procter, "and I declined the gift; but it was hard work to make Lamb believe that I was not in an impecunious condition."

Speaking of Lamb's sister Mary, Procter quoted Hazlitt's saying that "Mary Lamb was the most rational and wisest woman he had ever been acquainted with." As we went along some of the more retired streets in the old city, we had also, I remember, much gossip about Coleridge and his manner of reciting his poetry, especially when "Elia" happened to be among the listeners, for the philosopher put a high estimate upon Lamb's critical judgment. The author of "The Ancient Mariner" always had an excuse for any bad habit to which he was himself addicted, and he told Procter one day that perhaps snuff was the final cause of the human nose. In connection with Coleridge we had much reminiscence of such interesting persons as the Novellos, Martin Burney, Talfourd, and Crabb Robinson, and a store of anecdotes in which Haydon, Manning, Dyer, and Godwin figured at full length. In course of conversation I asked my companion if he thought Lamb had ever been really in love, and he told me interesting things of Hester Savory, a young Quaker girl of Pentonville, who inspired the poem embalming the name of Hester forever, and of Fanny Kelly, the actress with "the divine plain face," who will always live in one of "Elia's" most exquisite essays. "He had a *rev-*

erence for the sex," said Procter, "and there were tender spots in his heart that time could never entirely cover up or conceal."

During our walk we stepped into Christ's Hospital, and turned to the page on its record book where together we read this entry: "October 9, 1782, Charles Lamb, aged seven years, son of John Lamb, scrivener, and Elizabeth his wife."

It was a lucky morning when I dropped in to bid "good morrow" to the poet as I was passing his house one day, for it was then he took from among his treasures and gave to me an autograph letter addressed to himself by Charles Lamb in 1829. I found the dear old man alone and in his library, sitting at his books, with the windows wide open, letting in the spring odors. Quoting, as I entered, some lines from Wordsworth embalming May mornings, he began to talk of the older poets who had worshipped nature with the ardor of lovers, and his eyes lighted up with pleasure when I happened to remember some almost forgotten stanza from England's "Helicon." It was an easy transition from the old bards to "Elia," and he soon went on in his fine enthusiastic way to relate several anecdotes of his eccentric friend. As I rose to take leave he said, —

"Have I ever given you one of Lamb's letters to carry home to America?"

KEATS.

"No," I replied, "and you must not part with the least scrap of a note in 'Elia's' handwriting. Such things are too precious to be risked on a sea-voyage to another hemisphere."

"America ought to share with England in these things," he rejoined; and leading me up to a sort of cabinet in the library, he unlocked a drawer and got out a package of time-stained papers. "Ah," said he, as he turned over the golden leaves, "here is something you will like to handle." I unfolded the sheet, and lo! it was in Keats's handwriting, the sonnet on first looking into Chapman's Homer. "Keats gave it to me," said Procter, "many, many years ago," and then he proceeded to read, in tones tremulous with delight, these undying lines: —

> "Much have I travelled in the realms of gold,
> And many goodly states and kingdoms seen;
> Round many Western islands have I been
> Which bards in fealty to Apollo hold.
> Oft of one wide expanse had I been told
> That deep-browed Homer ruled as his demesne;
> Yet did I never breathe its pure serene
> Till I heard Chapman speak out loud and bold:
> Then felt I like some watcher of the skies
> When a new planet swims into his ken,
> Or like stout Cortez when with eagle eyes
> He stared at the Pacific — and all his men
> Looked at each other with a wild surmise —
> Silent, upon a peak in Darien."

I sat gazing at the man who had looked on Keats in the flush of his young genius, and wondered at my good fortune. As the living poet folded up again the faded manuscript of the illustrious dead one, and laid it reverently in its place, I felt grateful for the honor thus vouchsafed to a wandering stranger in a foreign land, and wished that other and worthier votaries of English letters might have been present to share with me the boon of such an interview. Presently my hospitable friend, still rummaging among the past, drew out a letter, which was the one, he said, he had been looking after. "Cram it into your pocket," he cried, "for I hear —— coming down stairs, and perhaps she won't let you carry it off!" The letter is addressed to B. W. Procter, Esq., 10 Lincoln's Inn, New Square. I give the entire epistle here just as it stands in the original which Procter handed me that memorable May morning. He told me that the law question raised in this epistle was a sheer fabrication of Lamb's, gotten up by him to puzzle his young correspondent, the conveyancer. The coolness ref rred to between himself and Robinson and Talfourd, Procter said, was also a fiction invented by Lamb to carry out his legal mystification.

Jan'y 19, 1829.

"MY DEAR PROCTER,--I am ashamed to have not taken the drift of your pleasant letter, which I find to have been pure invention. But jokes are not suspected in Bœotian Enfield. We are plain people, and our talk is of corn, and cattle, and Waltham markets. Besides I was a little out of sorts when I received it. The fact is, I am involved in a

case which has fretted me to death, and I have no reliance
except on you to extricate me. I am sure you will give me
your best legal advice, having no professional friend besides
but Robinson and Talfourd, with neither of whom at present
I am on the best terms. My brother's widow left a will,
made during the lifetime of my brother, in which I am
named sole Executor, by which she bequeaths forty acres
of arable property, which it seems she held under Covert
Baron, unknown to my Brother, to the heirs of the body of
Elizabeth Dowden, her married daughter by a first husband,
in fee simple, recoverable by fine — invested property,
mind, for there is the difficulty — subject to leet and quit
rent — in short, worded in the most guarded terms, to
shut out the property from Isaac Dowden the husband.
Intelligence has just come of the death of this person in
India, where he made a will, entailing this property (which
seem'd entangled enough already) to the heirs of his body,
that should not be born of his wife; for it seems by the
Law in India natural children can recover. They have put
the cause into Exchequer Process here, removed by Certio-
rari from the Native Courts, and the question is whether I
should as Executor, try the cause here, or again re-remove
to the Supreme Sessions at Bangalore, which I understand
I can, or plead a hearing before the Privy Council here.
As it involves all the little property of Elizabeth Dowden,
I am anxious to take the fittest steps, and what may be the
least expensive. For God's sake assist me, for the case is so
embarrassed that it deprives me of sleep and appetite. M.
Burney thinks there is a Case like it in Chapt. 170 Sect. 5
in Fearn's *Contingent Remainders.* Pray read it over with
him dispassionately, and let me have the result. The com-
plexity lies in the questionable power of the husband to
alienate in usum enfeoffments whereof he was only collater-
ally seized, etc."

[On the leaf at this place there are some words
in another hand. — F.]

"The above is some of M. Burney's memoranda, which he has left here, and you may cut out and give him. I had another favour to beg, which is the beggarliest of beggings. A few lines of verse for a young friend's Album (six will be enough). M. Burney will tell you who she is I want 'em for. A girl of gold. Six lines — make 'em eight — signed Barry C——. They need not be very good, as I chiefly want 'em as a foil to mine. But I shall be seriously obliged by any refuse scrap. We are in the last ages of the world, when St. Paul prophesied that women should be 'headstrong, lovers of their own wills, having Albums.' I fled hither to escape the Albumean persecution, and had not been in my new house 24 hours, when the Daughter of the next house came in with a friend's Album to beg a contribution, and the following day intimated she had one of her own. Two more have sprung up since. If I take the wings of the morning and fly unto the uttermost parts of the earth, there will Albums be. New Holland has Albums. But the age is to be complied with. M. B. will tell you the sort of girl I request the 10 lines for. Somewhat of a pensive cast what you admire. The lines may come before the Law question, as that can not be determined before Hilary Term, and I wish your deliberate judgment on that. The other may be flimsy and superficial. And if you have not burnt your returned letter pray re-send it me as a monumental token of my stupidity. 'T was a little unthinking of you to touch upon a sore subject. Why, by dabbling in those accursed Annuals I have become a byword of infamy all over the kingdom. I have sicken'd decent women for asking me to write in Albums. There be 'dark jests' abroad, Master Cornwall, and some riddles may live to be clear'd up. And 't is n't every saddle is put on the right steed. And forgeries and false Gospels are not peculiar to the age following the Apostles. And some tubs don't stand on their right bottom. Which is all I wish to say in these ticklish Times — and so your servant,

"Chs. Lamb."

LAMB.

At the age of seventy-seven Procter was invited to print his recollections of Charles Lamb, and his volume was welcomed in both hemispheres as a pleasant addition to "Eliana." During the last eighteen years of Lamb's life Procter knew him most intimately, and his chronicles of visits to the little gamboge-colored house in Enfield are charming pencillings of memory. When Lamb and his sister, tired of housekeeping, went into lodging and boarding with T—— W——, their sometime next-door neighbor — who, Lamb said, had one joke and forty pounds a year, upon which he retired in a green old age — Procter still kept up his friendly visits to his old associate. And after the brother and sister moved to their last earthly retreat in Edmonton, where Charles died in 1834, Procter still paid them regular visits of love and kindness. And after Charles's death, when Mary went to live at a house in St. John's Wood, her unfailing friend kept up his cheering calls there till she set out "for that unknown and silent shore," on the 20th of May, in 1847.

Procter's conversation was full of endless delight to his friends. His "asides" were sometimes full of exquisite touches. I remember one evening when Carlyle was present and rattling on against American institutions, half comic and half serious, Procter, who sat near me, kept up a constant underbreath of commentary, taking exactly the other side. Carlyle was full of horse-play over the character of George Washington, whom he never vouchsafed to call anything but George. He said our first President was a good surveyor, and knew how to measure timber, and that was about all. Procter kept whispering to me all the while Carlyle was discoursing, and going over Washington's fine traits to the disparagement of everything Carlyle was laying down as gospel. I was listening to both these distinguished men at the same time, and it was one of the most curious experiences in conversation I ever happened to enjoy.

I was once present when a loud-voiced person of quality, ignorant and supercilious, was inveighing against the want of taste commonly exhibited by artists when they chose their wives, saying they almost always selected inferior women. Procter, sitting next to me, put his hand on my shoulder, and, with a look expressive of ludicrous pity and contempt for the idiotic speaker, whispered, "And yet Vandyck married the daughter of Earl Gower, poor fellow!" The mock solemnity of Procter's manner was irresistible. It had a wink in it that really embodied the genius of fun and sarcasm.

Talking of the ocean with him one day, he revealed this curious fact: although he is the author of one of the most stirring and popular sea-songs in the language, —

"The sea, the sea, the open sea!" —

BROWNING.

he said he had rarely been upon the tossing element, having a great fear of being made ill by it. I think he told me he had never dared to cross the Channel even, and so had never seen Paris. He said, like many others, he delighted to gaze upon the waters from a safe place on land, but had a horror of living on it even for a few hours. I recalled to his recollection his own lines, —

> "I 'm on the sea! I 'm on the sea!
> I am where I would ever be," —

and he shook his head, and laughingly declared I must have misquoted his words, or that Dibdin had written the piece and put "Barry Cornwall's" signature to it. We had, I remember, a great deal of fun over the poetical lies, as he called them, which bards in all ages had perpetrated in their verse, and he told me some stories of English poets, over which we made merry as we sat together in pleasant Cavendish Square that summer evening.

His world-renowned song of "The Sea" he afterward gave me in his own handwriting, and it is still among my autographic treasures.

It was Procter who first in my hearing, twenty-five years ago, put such an estimate on the poetry of Robert Browning that I could not delay any longer to make acquaintance with his writings. I remember to have been startled at hearing the man who in his day had known so many poets declare that Browning was the peer of any one who had written in this century, and that, on the whole, his genius had not been excelled in his (Procter's) time. "Mind what I say," insisted Procter; "Browning will make an enduring name, and add another supremely great poet to England."

Procter could sometimes be prompted into describing that brilliant set of men and women who were in the habit of congregating at Lady Blessington's, and I well recollect his description of young N. P. Willis as he first appeared in her *salon*. "The young traveller came among us," said Procter, "enthusiastic, handsome, and good-natured, and took his place beside D'Orsay, Bulwer, Disraeli, and the other dandies as naturally as if he had been for years a London man about town. He was full of fresh talk concerning his own country, and we all admired his cleverness in compassing so aptly all the little newnesses of the situation. He was ready on all occasions, a little too ready, some of the *habitués* of the *salon* thought, and they could not understand his cool and quite-at-home manners. He became a favorite at first trial, and laid himself out determined to please and be pleased. His ever kind and thoughtful attention to others won him troops of friends, and I never can forget his unwearied goodness to a sick child of mine, with whom, night after night, he would sit by the bedside and watch, thus relieving the worn-out family in a way that was very tender and self-sacrificing."

WILLIS.

Of Lady Blessington's tact, kindness, and remarkable beauty Procter always spoke with ardor, and abated nothing from the popular idea of that fascinating person. He thought she had done more in her time to institute good feeling and social intercourse among men of letters than any other lady in England, and he gave her eminent credit for bringing forward the rising talent of the metropolis without waiting to be prompted by a public verdict. As the poet described her to me as she moved through her exquisite apartments, surrounded by all the luxuries that naturally connect themselves with one of her commanding position in literature and art, her radiant and exceptional beauty of person, her frank and cordial manners, the wit, wisdom, and grace of her speech, I thought of the fair Giovanna of Naples as painted in " Bianca Visconti " : —

> " Gods! what a light enveloped her!
> . . . . Her beauty
> Was of that order that the universe
> Seemed governed by her motion. . . . .
> The pomp, the music, the bright sun in heaven,
> Seemed glorious by her leave."

One of the most agreeable men in London literary society during Procter's time was the companionable and ever kind-hearted John Kenyon. He was a man compacted of all the best qualities of an incomparable good-nature. His friends used to call him " the apostle of cheerfulness." He could not endure a long face under his roof, and declined to see the dark side of anything. He wrote verses almost like a poet, but no one surpassed him in genuine admiration for whatever was excellent in others. No happiness was so great to him as the conferring of happiness on others, and I am glad to write myself his eternal debtor for much of my enjoyment in England, for he introduced me to many lifelong friendships, and he inaugurated for me much of that felicity which springs from intercourse with men and women whose books are the solace of our lifelong existence. How often have I seen Kenyon and Procter chirping together over an old quarto that had floated down from an early century, or rejoicing together over a well-worn letter in a family portfolio of treasures! They were a pair of veteran brothers, and there was never a flaw in their long and loving intercourse.

In a letter which Procter wrote to me in March, 1857, he thus refers to his old friend, then lately dead: "Everybody seems to be dying hereabouts, — one of my colleagues, one of my relations, one of my servants, three of them in one week, the last one in my own house. And now I seem fit for little else myself. My dear old friend Kenyon is dead. There never was a man, take him for all in all, with more amiable, attractive qualities. A kind friend, a good master, a generous and judicious dispenser of his wealth, honorable, sweet-tempered, and serene, and genial as a summer's day. It is true that he has left me a solid mark of his friendship. I did not expect anything; but if to like a man sincerely deserved such a mark of his regard, I deserved it. I doubt if he has left one person who really liked him more than I did. Yes, one — I think one — a woman. . . . . . I get old and weak and stupid. That pleasant journey to Niagara, that dip into your Indian summer, all such thoughts are over. I shall never see Italy; I shall never see Paris. My future is before me, — a very limited landscape, with scarcely one old friend left in it. I see a smallish room, with a bow-window looking south, a bookcase full of books, three or four drawings, and a library chair and table (once the property of my old friend Kenyon — I am writing on the table now), and you have the greater part of the vision before you. Is this the end of all things? I believe it is pretty much like most scenes in the fifth act, when the green (or black) curtain is about to drop and tell you that the play of *Hamlet* or of John Smith is over. But wait a little. There will be another piece, in which John Smith the younger will figure, and quite eclipse his old, stupid, wrinkled, useless, time-slaughtered parent. The king is dead, — long live the king!"

Kenyon was very fond of Americans, Professor Ticknor and Mr. George S. Hillard being especially dear to him. I remember hearing him say one day that the "best prepared" young foreigner he had ever met, who had come to see Europe, was Mr. Hillard. One day at his dinner-table, in the presence of Mrs. Jameson, Mr. and Mrs. Carlyle, Walter Savage Landor, Mr. and Mrs. Robert Browning, and the Procters, I heard him declare that one of the best talkers on any subject that might be started at the social board was the author of "Six Months in Italy."

It was at a breakfast in Kenyon's house that I first met Walter Savage Landor, whose writings are full of verbal legacies to posterity. As I entered the room with Procter, Landor was in the midst of an eloquent harangue on the high art of portraiture. Procter had been lately sitting to a daguerreotypist for a picture, and Mrs. Jameson, who was very fond of the poet, had arranged the camera for that occasion. Landor was holding the picture in his hand, declaring that it had never been surpassed as a specimen of that particular art. The grand-looking author of "Pericles and Aspasia" was standing in the middle of the room when we entered, and his voice sounded like an explosion of first-class artillery. Seeing Procter enter, he immediately began to address him compliments in high-sounding Latin. Poor modest Procter pretended to stop his ears that he might not listen to Landor's eulogistic phrases. Kenyon came to the rescue by declaring the breakfast had been waiting half an hour. When we ar-

LANDOR.

.

rived at the table Landor asked Procter to join him on an expedition into Spain which he was then contemplating. "No," said Procter, "for I cannot even 'walk Spanish,' and having never crossed the Channel, I do not intend to begin now."

"Never crossed the Channel!" roared Landor, — "never saw Napoleon Bonaparte!" He then began to tell us how the young Corsican looked when he first saw him, saying that he had the olive complexion and roundness of face of a Greek girl; that the consul's voice was deep and melodious, but untruthful in tone. While we were eating breakfast he went on to describe his Italian travels in early youth, telling us that he once saw Shelley and Byron meet in the doorway of a hotel in Pisa. Landor had lived in Italy many years, for he detested the climate of his native country, and used to say "one could only live comfortably in England who was rich enough to have a solar system of his own."

The Prince of Carpi said of Erasmus he was so thin-skinned that a fly would draw blood from him. The author of the "Imaginary Conversations" had the same infirmity. A very little thing would disturb him for hours, and his friends were never sure of his equanimity. I was present once when a blundering friend trod unwittingly on his favorite prejudice, and Landor went off instanter like a blaspheming torpedo. There were three things in the world which received no quarter at his hands, and when in the slightest degree he scented *hypocrisy*, *pharisaism*, or *tyranny*, straightway he became furious, and laid about him like a mad giant.

Procter told me that when Landor got into a passion, his rage was sometimes uncontrollable. The fiery spirit knew his weakness, but his anger quite overmastered him in spite of himself. " Keep your temper, Landor," somebody said to him one day when he was raging. "That is just what I don't wish to keep," he cried ; " I wish to be rid of such an infamous, ungovernable thing. I don't wish to *keep* my temper." Whoever wishes to get a good look at Landor will not seek for it alone in John Forster's interesting life of the old man, admirable as it is, but will turn to Dickens's " Bleak House" for side glances at the great author. In that vivid story Dickens has made his friend Landor sit for the portrait of Lawrence Boythorn. The very laugh that made the whole house vibrate, the roundness and fulness of voice, the fury of superlatives, are all given in Dickens's best manner, and no one who has ever seen Landor for half an hour could possibly mistake Boythorn for anybody else. Talking the matter over once with Dickens, he said, " Landor always took that presentation of himself in hearty good-humor, and seemed rather proud of the picture." This is Dickens's portrait : " He was not only a very handsome old gentleman, upright and stalwart, with a massive gray head, a fine composure of face when silent, a figure that might have become corpulent but for his being so continually in earnest that he gave it no rest, and a chin that might have subsided into a double chin but for the vehement emphasis in which it was constantly required to assist; but he was such a true gentleman in his manner, so chivalrously polite, his face was lighted by a smile of so much sweetness and tenderness, and it seemed so plain that he had nothing to hide, that really I could not help looking at him with equal pleasure, whether he smilingly conversed with Ada and me, or was led by Mr. Jarndyce into some great volley of superlatives, or threw up his head like a bloodhound, and gave out that tremendous Ha! ha! ha!"

Landor's energetic gravity, when he was proposing some colossal impossibility, the observant novelist would naturally seize on, for Dickens was always on the lookout for exaggerations in human language and conduct. It was at Procter's table I heard Dickens describe a scene which transpired after the publication of the "Old Curiosity Shop." It seems that the first idea of Little Nell occurred to Dickens when he was on a birthday visit to Landor, then living in Bath. The old man was residing in lodgings in St. James Square, in that city, and ever after connected Little Nell with that particular spot. No character in prose fiction was a greater favorite with Landor, and one day, years after the story was published, he burst out with a tremendous emphasis, and declared the one mistake of his life was that he had not purchased the house in Bath, and then and there burned it to the ground, so that no meaner association should ever desecrate the birthplace of Little Nell!

It was Procter's old schoolmaster (Dr. Drury, head-master of Harrow) who was the means of introducing Edmund Kean, the great actor, on the London stage. Procter delighted to recall the many theatrical triumphs of the eccentric tragedian, and the memoir which he printed of Kean will always be read with interest. I heard the poet one evening describe the player most graphically as he appeared in Sir Giles Overreach in 1816 at Drury Lane, when he produced such an effect on Lord Byron, who sat that night in a stage-box with Tom Moore. His lordship was so overcome by Kean's magnificent acting that he fell forward in a convulsive fit, and it was some time before he regained his wonted composure. Douglas Jerrold said that Kean's appearance in Shakespeare's Jew was like a chapter out of Genesis, and all who have seen the incomparable actor speak of his tiger-like power and infinite grace as unrivalled.

At Procter's house the best of England's celebrated men and women assembled, and it was a kind of enchantment to converse with the ladies one met there. It was indeed a privilege to be received by

MISS PROCTER.

the hostess herself, for Mrs. Procter was not only sure to be the most brilliant person among her guests, but she practised habitually that exquisite courtesy toward all which renders even a stranger, unwonted to London drawing-rooms, free from awkwardness and that constraint which are almost inseparable from a first appearance.

Among the persons I have seen at that house of urbanity in London I distinctly recall old Mrs. Montague, the mother of Mrs. Procter. She had met Robert Burns in Edinburgh when he first came up to that city to bring out his volume of poems. "I have seen many a handsome man in my time," said the old lady one day to us at dinner, "but never such a pair of eyes as young Robbie Burns kept flashing from under his beautiful brow." Mrs. Montague was much interested in Charles Sumner, and predicted for him all the eminence of his after-position. With a certain other American visitor she had no patience, and spoke of him to me as a "note of interrogation, too curious to be comfortable."

I distinctly recall Adelaide Procter as I first saw her on one of my early visits to her father's house. She was a shy, bright girl, and the poet drew my attention to her as she sat reading in a corner of the library. Looking at the young maiden, intent on her book, I remembered that exquisite sonnet in her father's volume, bearing date November, 1825, addressed to the infant just a month after her birth: —

"Child of my heart! My sweet, beloved First-born!
Thou dove who tidings bring'st of calmer hours!
Thou rainbow who dost shine when all the showers
Are past or passing! Rose which hath no thorn,
No spot, no blemish, — pure and unforlorn,
Untouched, untainted! O my Flower of flowers!
More welcome than to bees are summer bowers,
To stranded seamen life-assuring morn!
Welcome, a thousand welcomes! Care, who clings
Round all, seems loosening now its serpent fold:
New hope springs upward; and the bright world seems
Cast back into a youth of endless springs!
Sweet mother, is it so? or grow I old,
Bewildered in divine Elysian dreams?"

I whispered in the poet's ear my admiration of the sonnet and the beautiful subject of it as we sat looking at her absorbed in the volume on her knees. Procter, in response, murmured some words expressive of his joy at having such a gift from God to gladden his affectionate heart, and he told me afterward what a comfort Adelaide had always been to his household. He described to me a visit Wordsworth made to his house one day, and how gentle the old man's aspect was when he looked at the children. "He took the hand of my dear Adelaide in his," said Procter, "and spoke some words to her, the recollection of which helped, perhaps, with other things, to incline her to poetry." When a little child "the golden-tressed Adelaide," as the

WORDSWORTH.

poet calls her in one of his songs, must often have heard her father read aloud his own poems as they came fresh from the fount of song, and the impression no doubt wrought upon her young imagination a spell she could not resist. On a sensitive mind like hers such a piece as the "Petition to Time" could not fail of producing its full effect, and no girl of her temperament would be unmoved by the music of words like these:—

> "Touch us gently, Time!
>   Let us glide adown thy stream
> Gently, as we sometimes glide
>   Through a quiet dream.
> Humble voyagers are we,
> Husband, wife, and children three.
> (One is lost, an angel, fled
>   To the azure overhead.)
>
> "Touch us gently, Time!
>   We've not proud nor soaring wings:
> *Our* ambition, *our* content,
>   Lie in simple things.
> Humble voyagers are we,
> O'er Life's dim unsounded sea,
> Seeking only some calm clime:
>   Touch us *gently*, gentle Time!"

Adelaide Procter's name will always be sweet in the annals of English poetry. Her place was assured from the time when she made her modest advent, in 1853, in the columns of Dickens's "Household Words," and everything she wrote from that period onward until she died gave evidence of **striking** and **peculiar talent.** I have heard Dickens **describe how** she first began **to proffer contributions to his** columns over a feigned name, that **of Miss Mary Berwick; how he** came to think that **his unknown** correspondent **must be a** governess; **how, as** time **went on, he learned to** value his new contributor for her **self-reliance and** punctuality,— **qualities upon which Dickens always** placed **a** high **value; how at last, going to dine one** day with his **old friends the Procters, he launched** enthusiastically **out in praise of Mary** Berwick (**the writer herself, Adelaide Procter,** sitting at the table); **and how the** delighted **mother,** being in **the secret, revealed,** with tears **of joy, the** real name **of the** young **aspirant.** Although Dickens has told the **whole story most feelingly in an** introduction to Miss **Procter's " Legends and Lyrics,"** issued after her **death, to hear it from his own li**ps and sympathetic **heart, as I have done, was, as may** be imagined, **something better even than** reading his pathetic **words on the printed page.**

One of the most interesting ladies **in** London **literary society in the period of which I** am writing **was Mrs. Jameson, the dear and** honored friend of **Procter and his family.** During many years of her **later life she stood in the relation of** consoler to her **sex in** England. Women **in** mental anguish needing consolation **and** counsel fled **to her** as to a convent **for protection and** guidance. **Her** published writ-

MRS JAMESON.

ings established such a claim upon her sympathy in the hearts of her readers that much of her time for twenty years before she died was spent in helping others, by correspondence and personal contact, to submit to the sorrows God had cast upon them. She believed, with Milton, that it is miserable enough to be blind, but still more miserable not to be able to bear blindness. Her own earlier life had been darkened by griefs, and she knew from a deep experience what it was to enter the cloud and stand waiting and hoping in the shadows. In her instructive and delightful society I spent many an hour twenty years ago in the houses of Procter and Rogers and Kenyon. Procter, knowing my admiration of the Kemble family, frequently led the conversation up to that regal line which included so many men and women of genius. Mrs. Jameson was never weary of being questioned as to the legitimate supremacy of Mrs. Siddons and her nieces, Fanny and Adelaide Kemble. While Rogers talked of Garrick, and Procter of Kean, she had no enthusiasms that were not bounded in by those fine spirits whom she had watched and worshipped from her earliest years.

Now and then in the garden of life we get that special bite out of the sunny side of a peach. One of my own memorable experiences in that way came in this wise. I had heard, long before I went abroad, so much of the singing of the youngest child of the "Olympian dynasty," Adelaide Kemble, so much of a brief career crowded with triumphs on the lyric stage, that I longed, if it might be possible, to listen to "the true daughter of her race." The rest of her family for years had been, as it were, "nourished on Shakespeare," and achieved greatness in that high walk of genius; but now came one who could interpret Mozart, Bellini, and Mercadante, one who could equal what Pasta and Malibran and Persiani and Grisi had taught the world to understand and worship. "Ah!" said a friend, "if you could only hear *her* sing 'Casta Diva!'" "Yes," said another, "and 'Auld Robin Gray!'" No wonder, I thought, at the universal enthusiasm for a vocal and lyrical artist who can alternate with equal power from "Casta Diva" to "Auld Robin Gray." I *must* hear her! She had left the stage, after a brief glory upon it, but as Madame Sartoris she sometimes sang at home to her guests.

"We are invited to hear some music this evening," said Procter to me one day, "and you must go with us." I went, and our hostess was the once magnificent *prima donna!* At intervals throughout the evening, with a voice

"That crowds and hurries and precipitates
With thick fast warble its delicious notes,"

she poured out her full soul in melody. We all know her now as the author of that exquisite

"Week in a French Country-House," and her fascinating book somehow always mingles itself in my memory with the enchanted evening when I heard her sing. As she sat at the piano in all her majestic beauty, I imagined her a sort of later St. Cecilia, and could have wished for another Raphael to paint her worthily. Henry Chorley, who was present on that memorable evening, seemed to be in a kind of nervous rapture at hearing again the supreme and willing singer. Procter moved away into a dim corner of the room, and held his tremulous hand over his eyes. The old poet's sensitive spirit seemed at times to be going out on the breath of the glorious artist who was thrilling us all with her power. Mrs. Jameson bent forward to watch every motion of her idol, looking applause at every noble passage. Another lady, whom I did not know, was tremulous with excitement, and I could well imagine what might have taken place when the "impassioned chantress" sang and enacted Semiramide as I have heard it described. Every one present was inspired by her fine mien, as well as by her transcendent voice. Mozart, Rossini, Bellini, Cherubini, — how she flung herself that night, with all her gifts, into their highest compositions! As she rose and was walking away from the piano, after singing an air from the "Medea" with a pathos that no musically uneducated pen like mine can or ought to attempt a description of, some one intercepted her and whispered a request. Again she turned, and walked toward the instrument like a queen among her admiring court. A flash of lightning, followed by a peal of thunder that jarred the house, stopped her for a moment on her way to the piano. A sudden summer tempest was gathering, and crash after crash made it impossible for her to begin. As she stood waiting for the "elemental fury" to subside, her attitude was quite worthy of the niece of Mrs. Siddons. When the thunder had grown less frequent, she threw back her beautiful classic head and touched the keys. The air she had been called upon to sing was so wild and weird, a dead silence fell upon the room, and an influence as of terror pervaded the whole assembly. It was a song by Dessauer, which he had composed for her voice, the words by Tennyson. No one who was present that evening can forget how she broke the silence with

"We were two daughters of one race,"

or how she uttered the words,

"The wind is roaring in turret and tree."

It was like a scene in a great tragedy, and then I fully understood the worship she had won as belonging only to those consummate artists who have arisen to dignify and ennoble the lyric stage. As we left the house Procter said, "You are in great luck to-night. I never heard her sing more divinely."

The Poet frequently spoke to me of the old days when he was contributing to the "London Magazine," which fifty years ago was deservedly so popular in Great Britain. All the "best talent" (to use a modern advertisement phrase) wrote for it. Carlyle sent his papers on Schiller to be printed in it; De Quincey's "Confessions of an English Opium-Eater" appeared in its pages; and the essays of "Elia" came out first in that potent periodical; Landor, Keats, and John Bowring contributed to it; and to have printed a prose or poetical article in the "London" entitled a man to be asked to dine out anywhere in society in those days. In 1821 the proprietors began to give dinners in Waterloo Place once a month to their contributors, who, after the cloth was removed, were expected to talk over the prospects of the magazine, and lay out the contents for next month. Procter described to me the authors of his generation as they sat round the old "mahogany-tree" of that period. "Very social and expansive hours they passed in that pleasant room half a century ago. Thither came stalwart Allan Cunningham, with his Scotch face shining with good-nature; Charles Lamb, 'a Diogenes with the heart of a St. John'; Hamilton Reynolds, whose good temper and vivacity were like condiments at a feast; John

Clare, the peasant-poet, simple as a daisy; Tom Hood, young, silent, and grave, but who nevertheless now and then shot out a pun that damaged the shaking sides of the whole company; De Quincey, self-involved and courteous, rolling out his periods with a pomp and splendor suited, perhaps, to a high Roman festival; and with these sons of fame gathered certain nameless folk whose contributions to the great 'London' are now under the protection of that tremendous power which men call *Oblivion*."

It was a vivid pleasure to hear Procter describe Edward Irving, the eccentric preacher, who made such a deep impression on the spirit of his time. He is now dislimned into space, but he was, according to all his thoughtful contemporaries, a "son of thunder," a "giant force of activity." Procter fully indorsed all that Carlyle has so nobly written of the eloquent man who, dying at forty-two, has stamped his strong personal vitality on the age in which he lived.

Procter, in his younger days, was evidently much impressed by that clever rascal who, under the name of "Janus Weathercock," scintillated at intervals in the old "London Magazine." Wainwright — for that was his real name — was so brilliant, he made friends for a time among many of the first-class contributors to that once famous periodical; but the Ten Commandments ruined all his prospects for life. A murderer, a forger, a thief, — in short, a sinner in general, — he came to grief rather early in his wicked career, and suffered penalties of the law accordingly, but never to the full extent of his remarkable deserts. I have heard Procter describe his personal appearance as he came sparkling into the room, clad in undress military costume. His smart conversation deceived those about him into the belief that he had been an officer in the dragoons, that he had spent a large fortune, and now condescended to take a part in periodical literature with the culture of a gentleman and the grace of an amateur. How this vapid charlatan in a braided surtout and prismatic necktie could so long veil his real character from, and retain the regard of, such men as Procter and Talfourd and Coleridge is amazing. Lamb calls him the "kind and light-hearted Janus," and thought he liked him. The contributors often spoke of his guileless nature at the festal monthly board of the magazine, and no one dreamed that this gay and mock-smiling London cavalier was about to begin a career so foul and monstrous that the annals of crime for centuries have no blacker pages inscribed on them. To secure the means of luxurious living without labor, and to pamper his dandy tastes, this lounging, lazy *littérateur* resolved to become a murderer on a large scale, and accompany his cruel poisonings with forgeries whenever they were most convenient. His custom for years was to effect policies of insurance on the lives of his relations, and then at the proper time administer strychnine to his victims. The heart sickens at the recital of his brutal crimes. On the life of a beautiful young girl named Abercrombie this fiendish wretch effected an insurance at various offices for £18,000 before he sent her to her account with the rest of his poisoned too-confiding relatives. So many heavily insured ladies dying in violent convulsions drew attention to the gentleman who always called to collect the money. But why this consummate criminal was not brought to justice and hung, my Lord Abinger never satisfactorily divulged. At last this polished Sybarite, who boasted that he always drank the richest Montepulciano, who could not sit long in a room that was not garlanded with flowers, who said he felt lonely in an apartment without a fine cast of the Venus de' Medici in it,—this self-indulgent voluptuary at last committed several forgeries on the Bank of England, and the Old Bailey sessions of July, 1837, sentenced him to transportation for life. While he was lying in Newgate prior to his departure, with other convicts, to New South Wales, where he died, Dickens went with a former acquaintance of the prisoner to see him. They found him still possessed with a morbid self-esteem and a poor and empty vanity. All other feelings and interests were overwhelmed

HUNT.

by an excessive idolatry of self, and he claimed (I now quote his own words to Dickens) a soul whose nutriment is love, and its offspring art, music, divine song, and still holier philosophy. To the last this super-refined creature seemed undisturbed by remorse. What place can we fancy for such a reptile, and what do we learn from such a career? Talfourd has so wisely summed up the whole case for us that I leave the dark tragedy with the recital of this solemn sentence from a paper on the culprit in the "Final Memorials of Charles Lamb": "Wainwright's vanity, nurtured by selfishness and unchecked by religion, became a disease, amounting perhaps to monomania, and yielding one lesson to repay the world for his existence, viz. that there is no state of the soul so dangerous as that in which the vices of the sensualist are envenomed by the grovelling intellect of the scorner."

One of the men best worth meeting in London, under any circumstances, was Leigh Hunt, but it was a special boon to find him and Procter together. I remember a day in the summer of 1859 when Procter had a party of friends at dinner to meet Hawthorne, who was then on a brief visit to London. Among the guests were the Countess of ———, Kinglake, the author of "Eothen," Charles Sumner, then on his way to Paris, and Leigh Hunt, the mercurial qualities of whose blood were even then perceptible in his manner.

Adelaide Procter did not reach home in season to begin the dinner with us, but she came later in the evening, and sat for some time in earnest talk with Hawthorne. It was a "goodly companie," long to be remembered. Hunt and Procter were in a mood for gossip over the ruddy port. As the twilight deepened around the table, which was exquisitely decorated with flowers, the author of "Rimini" recalled to Procter's recollection other memorable tables where they used to meet in vanished days with Lamb, Coleridge, and others of their set long since passed away. As they talked on in rather low tones, I saw the two old poets take hands more than once at the mention of dead and beloved names. I recollect they had a good deal of fine talk over the great singers whose voices had delighted them in bygone days; speaking with rapture of Pasta, whose tones in opera they thought incomparably the grandest musical utterances they had ever heard. Procter's tribute in verse to this

"Queen and wonder of the enchanted world of sound"

is one of his best lyrics, and never was singer more divinely complimented by poet. At the dinner I am describing he declared that she walked on the stage like an empress. "And when she sang," said he, "I held my breath." Leigh Hunt, in one of his letters to Procter in 1831, says: "As to Pasta, I love her, for she makes the ground firm under my feet, and the sky blue over my head."

I cannot remember all the good things I heard that day, but some of them live in my recollection still. Hunt quoted Hartley Coleridge, who said, "No boy ever imagined himself a poet while he was reading Shakespeare or Milton." And speaking of Landor's oaths, he said, "They are so rich, they are really nutritious." Talking of criticism, he said he did not believe in spiteful imps, but in kindly elves who would "nod to him and do him courtesies." He laughed at Bishop Berkely's attempt to destroy the world in one octavo volume. His doctrine to mankind always was, "Enlarge your tastes, that you may enlarge your hearts." He believed in reversing original propensities by education, — as Spallanzani brought up eagles on bread and milk, and fed doves on raw meat. "Don't let us demand too much of human nature," was a line in his creed; and he believed in Hood's advice, that gentleness in a case of wrong direction is always better than vituperation.

> "Mid light, and by degrees, should be the plan
>   To cure the dark and erring mind;
>   But who would rush at a benighted man
>   And give him two black eyes for being blind?"

I recollect there was much converse that day on the love of reading in old age, and Leigh Hunt observed that Sir Robert Walpole, seeing Mr. Fox busy in the library at Houghton, said to him: "And you can read! Ah, how I envy you! I totally neglected the *habit* of reading when I was young, and now in my old age I cannot read a single page." Hunt himself was a man who could be "penetrated by a book." It was inspiring to hear him dilate over "Plutarch's Morals," and quote passages from that delightful essay on "The Tranquillity of the Soul." He had such reverence for the wisdom folded up on his library shelves, he declared that the very perusal of the *backs of his books* was "a discipline of humanity." Whenever and wherever I met this charming person, I learned a lesson of gentleness and patience; for, steeped to the lips in poverty as he was, he was ever the most cheerful, the most genial companion and friend. He never left his good-nature outside the family circle, as a Mussulman leaves his slippers outside a mosque, but he always brought a smiling face into the house with him. T—— A——, whose fine floating wit has never yet quite condensed itself into a star, said one day of a Boston man that he was "east-wind made flesh." Leigh Hunt was exactly the opposite of this; he was compact of all the spicy breezes that blow. In his bare cottage at Hammersmith the temperament of his fine spirit heaped up such riches of fancy that kings, if wise ones, might envy his magic power.

"Onward in faith, and leave the rest to Heaven," was a line he often quoted. There was about him such a modest fortitude in want and poverty, such an inborn mental superiority to low and uncomfortable circumstances, that he rose without effort into a region encompassed with felicities, untroubled by a care or sorrow. He always reminded me of that favorite child of the genii who carried an amulet in his bosom by which all the gold and jewels of the Sultan's halls were no sooner beheld than they became his own. If he sat down companionless to a solitary chop, his imagination transformed it straightway into a fine shoulder of mutton. When he looked out of his dingy old windows on the four bleak elms in front of his dwelling, he saw, or thought he saw, a vast forest, and he could hear in the note of one poor sparrow even the silvery voices of a hundred nightingales. Such a man might often be cold and hungry, but he had the wit never to be aware of it.

Hunt's love for Procter was deep and tender, and in one of his notes to me he says, referring to the meeting my memory has been trying to describe, "I have reasons for liking our dear friend Procter's wine beyond what you saw when we dined together at his table the other day." Procter prefixed a memoir of the life and writings of Ben Jonson to the great dramatist's works printed by Moxon in 1838. I happen to be the lucky owner of a copy of this edition that once belonged to Leigh Hunt, who has enriched it and perfumed the pages, as it were, by his annotations. The memoir abounds in felicities of expression, and is the best brief chronicle yet made of rare Ben and his poetry. Leigh Hunt has filled the margins with his own neat handwriting, and as I turn over the leaves, thus companioned, I seem to meet those two loving brothers in modern song, and have again the benefit of their sweet society, — a society redolent of

> "The love of learning, the sequestered nooks,
> And all the sweet serenity of books."

I shall not soon forget the first morning I walked with Procter and Kenyon to the famous house No. 22 St. James Place, overlooking the Green Park, to a breakfast with Samuel Rogers. Mixed up with this matutinal rite was much that belongs to the modern literary and political history of England. Fox, Burke, Talleyrand, Grattan, Walter Scott, and many other great ones have sat there and held converse on divers matters with the banker-poet. For more than half a century the wits and the wise men honored that unpretending mansion with their presence. On my way thither for the first time my companions related anecdote after anecdote of the "ancient bard," as they called our host, telling me also how all his life long the poet of Memory had been giving substantial aid to poor authors; how he had befriended Sheridan, and how good he had been to Campbell in his sorest needs. Intellectual or artistic excellence was a sure passport to his *salon*, and his door never turned on reluctant hinges to

ROGERS.

admit the unfriended man of letters who needed his aid and counsel.

We arrived in quite an expectant mood, to find our host already seated at the head of his table, and his good man Edmund standing behind his chair. As we entered the room, and I saw Rogers sitting there so venerable and strange, I was reminded of that line of Wordsworth's,

"The oldest man he seemed that ever wore gray hair."

But old as he was, he seemed full of *verve*, vivacity, and decision. Knowing his homage for Ben Franklin, I had brought to him as a gift from America an old volume issued by the patriot printer in 1741. He was delighted with my little present, and began at once to say how much he thought of Franklin's prose. He considered the style admirable, and declared that it might be studied now for improvement in the art of composition. One of the guests that morning was the Rev. Alexander Dyce, the scholarly editor of Beaumont and Fletcher, and he very soon drew Rogers out on the subject of Warren Hastings's trial. It seemed ghostly enough to hear that famous event depicted by one who sat in the great hall of William Rufus; who day after day had looked on and listened to the eloquence of Fox and Sheridan; who had heard Edmund Burke raise his voice till the old arches of Irish oak resounded, and impeach Warren Hastings, "in the name of both sexes, in the name of every age, in the name of every rank, as the common enemy and oppressor of all." It thrilled me to hear Rogers say, "As I walked up Parliament Street with Mrs. Siddons, after hearing Sheridan's great speech, we both agreed that never before could human lips have uttered more eloquent words." That morning Rogers described to us the appearance of Grattan as he first saw and heard him when he made his first speech in Parliament. "Some of us were inclined to laugh," said he, "at the orator's Irish brogue when he began his speech that day, but after he had been on his legs five minutes nobody dared to laugh any more." Then followed personal anecdotes of Madame De Stael, the Duke of Wellington, Walter Scott, Tom Moore, and Sydney Smith, all exquisitely told. Both our host and his friend Procter had known or entertained most of the celebrities of their day. Procter soon led the conversation up to matters connected with the stage, and thinking of John Kemble and Edmund Kean, I ventured to ask Rogers who of all the great actors he had seen bore away the palm. "I have looked upon a magnificent procession of them," he said, "in my time, and I never saw any one superior to *David Garrick*." He then repeated Hannah More's couplet on receiving as a gift from Mrs. Garrick the shoe-buckles which once belonged to the great actor: —

> "Thy buckles, O Garrick, another may use,
> But none shall be found who can tread in thy shoes."

We applauded his memory and his manner of reciting the lines, which seemed to please him. "How much can sometimes be put into an epigram!" he said to Procter, and asked him if he remembered the lines about Earl Grey and the Kaffir war. Procter did not recall them, and Rogers set off again : —

> "A dispute has arisen of late at the Cape,
> As touching the devil, his color and shape;
> While some folks contend that the devil is white,
> The others aver that he's black as midnight;
> But now 't is decided quite right in this way,
> And all are convinced that the devil is *Grey*."

We asked him if he remembered the theatrical excitement in London when Garrick and his troublesome contemporary, Barry, were playing King Lear at rival houses, and dividing the final opinion of the critics. "Yes," said he, "perfectly. I saw both those wonderful actors, and fully agreed at the time with the admirable epigram that ran like wildfire into every nook and corner of society." "Did the epigram still live in his memory?" we asked. The old man seemed looking across the misty valley of time for a few moments, and then gave it without a pause : —

> "The town have chosen different ways
> To praise their different Lears;
> To Barry they give loud applause,
> To Garrick only tears."

> "A king! ay, every inch a king,
> Such Barry doth appear;
> But Garrick's quite another thing,—
> He's every inch *King Lear!*"

Among other things which Rogers told us that morning, I remember he had much to say of Byron's *forgetfulness* as to all manner of things. As an evidence of his inaccuracy, Rogers related how the noble bard had once quoted to him some lines on Venice as Southey's "which he wanted me to admire," said Rogers; "and as I wrote them myself, I had no hesitation in doing so. The lines are in my poem on Italy, and begin,

> "'There is a glorious city in the sea.'"

Samuel Lawrence had recently painted in oils a portrait of Rogers, and we asked to see it; so Edmund was sent up stairs to get it, and bring it to the table. Rogers himself wished to compare it with his own face, and had a looking-glass held before him. We sat by in silence as he regarded the picture attentively, and waited for his criticism. Soon he burst out with, "Is my nose so d——y sharp as that?" We all exclaimed, "No! no! the artist is at fault there, sir." "I thought so," he cried; "he has painted the face of a dead man, d—n him!" Some one said, "The portrait is too hard." "I won't be painted as a hard man," rejoined Rogers. "I am not a hard man, am I, Procter?" asked the old poet. Procter deprecated with energy such an idea as that. Looking at the portrait again, Rogers said, with great feeling, " Children would run away from that face, and they never ran away from me ! " Notwithstanding all he had to say against the portrait, I thought it a wonderful likeness, and a painting of great value. Moxon, the publisher, who was present, asked for a certain portfolio of engraved heads which had been made from time to time of Rogers, and this was brought and opened for our examination of its contents. Rogers insisted upon looking over the portraits, and he amused us by his cutting comments on each one as it came out of the portfolio. " This," said he, holding one up, " is the head of a cunning fellow, and this the face of a debauched clergyman, and this the visage of a shameless drunkard ! " After a comic discussion of the pictures of himself, which went on for half an hour, he said, " It is time to change the topic, and set aside the little man for a very great one. Bring me my collection of Washington portraits." These were brought in, and he had much to say of American matters. He remembered being told, when a boy, by his father one day, that " a fight had recently occurred at a place called Bunker Hill, in America." He then inquired about Webster and the monument. He had met Webster in England, and greatly admired him. Now and then his memory was at fault, and he spoke occasionally of events as still existing which had happened half a century before. I remember what a shock it gave me when he asked me if Alexander Hamilton had printed any new pamphlets lately, and begged me to send him anything that distinguished man might publish after I got home to America.

I recollect how delighted I was when Rogers sent me an invitation the second time to breakfast with him. On that occasion the poet spoke of being in Paris on a pleasure-tour with Daniel Webster, and he grew eloquent over the great American orator's genius. He also referred with enthusiasm to Bryant's poetry, and quoted with deep feeling the first three verses of " The Future Life." When he pronounced the lines : —

> " My name on earth was ever in thy prayer,
> And must thou never utter it in heaven ? "

his voice trembled, and he faltered out, " I cannot go on: there is something in that poem which breaks me down, and I must never try again to recite verses so full of tenderness and undying love."

For Longfellow's poems, then just published in England, he expressed the warmest admiration, and thought the author of " Voices of the Night " one of the most perfect artists in English verse who had ever lived.

Rogers's reminiscences of Holland House that morning were a series of delightful pictures painted by an artist who left out none of the salient features, but gave to everything he touched a graphic reality. In his narrations the eloquent men, the fine ladies, he had seen there assembled again around their noble host and hostess, and one listened in the pleasant breakfast-room in St. James Place to the wit and wisdom of that brilliant company which met fifty years ago in the great *salon* of that princely mansion, which will always be famous in the literary and political history of England.

Rogers talked that morning with inimitable finish and grace of expression. A light seemed to play over his faded features when he recalled some happy past experience, and his eye would sometimes fill as he glanced back among his kindred, all now dead save one, his sister, who also lived to a great age. His head was very fine, and I never could quite understand the satirical sayings about his personal appearance which have crept into the literary gossip of his time. He was by no means the vivacious spectre some of his contemporaries have represented him, and I never thought of connecting him with that terrible line in "The Mirror of Magistrates," —

"His withered fist still striking at Death's door."

His dome of brain was one of the amplest and most perfectly shaped I ever saw, and his countenance was very far from unpleasant. His faculties to enjoy had not perished with age. He certainly looked like a well-seasoned author, but not dropping to pieces yet. His turn of thought was characteristic, and in the main just, for he loved the best, and was naturally impatient of what was low and mean in conduct and intellect. He had always lived in an atmosphere of art, and his reminiscences of painters and sculptors were never wearisome or dull. He had a store of pleasant anecdotes of Chantrey, whom he had employed as a wood-carver long before he became a modeller in clay; and he had also much to tell us of Sir Joshua Reynolds, whose lectures he had attended, and whose studio-talk had been familiar to him while he was a young man and studying art himself as an amateur. It was impossible almost to make Rogers seem a real being as we used to surround his table during those mornings and sometimes deep into the afternoons. We were listening to one who had talked with Boswell about Dr. Johnson; who had sat hours with Mrs. Piozzi; who read the "Vicar of Wakefield" the day it was published; who had heard Haydn, the composer, playing at a concert, "dressed out with a sword"; who had listened to Talleyrand's best sayings from his own lips; who had seen John Wesley lying dead in his coffin, "an old man, with the countenance of a little child"; who had been with Beckford at Fonthill; who had seen Porson slink back into the dining-room after the company had left it and drain what was left in the wineglasses; who had crossed the Apennines with Byron; who had seen Beau Nash in the height of his career dancing minuets at Bath; who had known Lady Hamilton in her days of beauty, and seen her often with Lord Nelson; who was in Fox's room when that great man lay dying; and who could describe Pitt from personal observation, speaking always as if his mouth was "full of worsted." It was unreal as a dream to sit there in St. James Place and hear that old man talk by the hour of what one had been reading about all one's life. One thing, I must confess, somewhat shocked me, — I was not prepared for the feeble manner in which some of Rogers's best stories were received by the gentlemen who had gathered at his table on those Tuesday mornings. But when Procter told me in explanation afterward that they had all "heard the same anecdotes every week, perhaps, for half a century from the same lips," I no longer wondered at the seeming apathy I had witnessed. It was a great treat to me, however, the talk I heard at Rogers's hospitable table, and my three visits there cannot be erased from the pleasantest tablets of memory. There is only one regret connected with them, but that loss still haunts me. On one of those memorable mornings I was obliged to leave earlier than the rest of the company on account of an engagement out of London, and Lady Beecher (formerly

Miss O'Neil), the great actress of other days, came in and read an hour to the old poet and his guests. Procter told me afterward that among other things she read, at Rogers's request, the 14th chapter of Isaiah, and that her voice and manner seemed like inspiration.

Seeing and talking with Rogers was, indeed, like living in the past: and one may imagine how weird it seemed to a raw Yankee youth, thus facing the man who might have shaken hands with Dr. Johnson. I ventured to ask him one day if he had ever seen the doctor. "No," said he, "but I went down to Bolt Court in 1782 with the intention of making Dr. Johnson's acquaintance. I raised the knocker tremblingly, and hearing the shuffling footsteps as of an old man in the entry, my heart failed me, and I put down the knocker softly again, and crept back into Fleet Street without seeing the vision I was not bold enough to encounter." I thought it was something to have heard the footsteps of old Sam Johnson stirring about in that ancient entry, and for my own part I was glad to look upon the man whose ears had been so strangely privileged.

Rogers drew about him all the musical as well as the literary talent of London. Grisi and Jenny Lind often came of a morning to sing their best *arias* to him when he became too old to attend the opera; and both Adelaide and Fanny Kemble brought to

LESLIE.

him frequently the rich tributes of their genius in art.

It was my good fortune, through the friendship of Procter, to make the acquaintance, at Rogers's table, of Leslie, the artist, — a warm friend of the old poet, — and to be taken round by him and shown all the principal private galleries in London. He first drew my attention to the pictures by Constable, and pointed out their quiet beauty to my uneducated eye, thus instructing me to hate all those intemperate landscapes and lurid compositions which abound in the shambles of modern art. In the company of Leslie I saw my first Titians and Vandycks, and felt, as Northcote says, on my good behavior in the presence of portraits so lifelike and inspiring. It was Leslie who inoculated me with a love of Gainsborough, before whose perfect pictures a spectator involuntarily raises his hat and stands uncovered. (And just here let me advise every art lover who goes to England to visit the little Dulwich Gallery, only a few miles from London, and there to spend an hour or two among the exquisite Gainsboroughs. No small collection in Europe is better worth a visit, and the place itself in summer-time is enchanting with greenery.)

As Rogers's dining-room abounded in only first-rate works of art, Leslie used to take round the guests and make us admire the Raphaels and Correggios. Inserted in the walls on each side of the mantel-piece, like tiles, were several of Turner's original oil and water-color drawings, which that supreme artist had designed to illustrate Rogers's "Poems" and "Italy." Long before Ruskin made those sketches world-famous in his "Modern Painters," I have heard Leslie point out their beauties with as fine an enthusiasm. He used to say that they purified the whole atmosphere round St. James Place!

Procter had a genuine regard for Count d'Orsay, and he pointed him out to me one day sitting in the window of his club, near Gore House, looking out on Piccadilly. The count seemed a little past his prime, but was still the handsomest man in London. Procter described him as a brilliant person, of special ability, and by no means a mere dandy.

I first saw Procter's friend, John Forster, the biographer of Goldsmith and Dickens, in his pleasant rooms, No. 58 Lincoln's Inn Fields. He was then in his prime, and looked brimful of energy. His age might have been forty, or a trifle onward from that mile-stone, and his whole manner announced a determination to assert that nobody need prompt *him*. His voice rang loud and clear, up stairs and down, everywhere throughout his premises. When he walked over the uncarpeted floor, you *heard* him walk, and he meant you should. When *he* spoke, nobody required an ear-trumpet; the deaf never

D'ORSAY.

lost a syllable of his manly utterances. Procter and he were in the same Commission, and were on excellent terms, the younger officer always regarding the elder with a kind of leonine deference.

It was to John Forster these charming lines were addressed by Barry Cornwall, when the poet sent his old friend a present of Shakespeare's Works. A more exquisite compliment was never conveyed in verse so modest and so perfect in simple grace :—

> "I do not know a man who better reads
> Or weighs the great thoughts of the book I send, —
> Better than he whom I have called my friend
> For twenty years and upwards. He who feeds
> Upon Shakesperian pastures never needs
> The humbler food which springs from plains below;
> Yet may he love the little flowers that blow,
> And him excuse who for their beauty pleads.
>
> "Take then my Shakespeare to some sylvan nook;
> And pray thee, in the name of Days of old,
> Good-will and friendship, never bought or sold,
> Give me assurance thou wilt always look
> With kindness still on Spirits of humbler mould;
> Kept firm by resting on that wondrous book,
> Wherein the Dream of Life is all unrolled."

Forster's library was filled with treasures, and he brought to the dinner-table, the day I was first with him, such rare and costly manuscripts and annotated volumes to show us, that one's appetite for "made dishes" was quite taken away. The excellent lady whom he afterward married was one of the guests, and among the gentlemen present I remember the brilliant author of "The Bachelor of the Albany," a book that was then the Novel sensation in London. Forster flew from one topic to another with admirable skill, and entertained us with anecdotes of Wellington and Rogers, gilding the time with capital imitations of his celebrated contemporaries in literature and on the stage. A touch about Edmund Kean made us all start from our chairs and demand a mimetic repetition. Forster must have been an excellent private actor, for he had power and skill quite exceptional in that way. His force carried him along wherever he chose to go, and when he played "Kitely," his ability must have been strikingly apparent. After his marriage, and when he removed from Lincoln's Inn to his fine residence at "Palace-Gate House," he gave frequent readings, evincing remarkable natural and acquired talents. For Dickens he had a love amounting to jealousy. He never quite relished anybody else whom the great novelist had a fondness for, and I have heard droll stories touching this weakness. For Professor Felton he had unbounded regard, which had grown up by correspondence and through report from Dickens. He had never met Felton, and when the professor arrived in London, Dickens, with his love of fun, arranged a bit of cajolery, which was never quite forgotten, though wholly forgiven. Knowing how highly Forster esteemed Felton, through his writings and his letters, Dickens resolved to take Felton at once to Forster's house and introduce him as *Professor Stowe*, the port of both these gentlemen being pretty nearly equal. The Stowes were then in England on their triumphant tour, and this made the attempt at deception an easy one. So, Felton being in the secret, he and Dickens proceed to Forster's house and are shown in. Down comes Forster into the library, and is presented forthwith to "*Professor Stowe*." "Uncle Tom's Cabin" is at once referred to, and the talk goes on in that direction for some time. At last both Dickens and Felton fell into such a paroxysm of laughter at Forster's dogged determination to be complimentary to the world-renowned novel, that they could no longer hold out; and Forster, becoming almost insane with wonder at the hilarious conduct of his two visitors, Dickens revealed their wickedness, and a right jolly day the happy trio made of it.

Talfourd informs us that Forster had become to Charles Lamb as one of his oldest campanions, and that Mary also cherished a strong regard for him. It is surely a proof of his admirable qualities that the love of so many of England's best and greatest was secured to him by so lasting a tenure. To have the friendship of Landor, Dickens, and Procter through long years; to have Carlyle for a constant votary, and to be mourned by him with an abiding sorrow, — these are no slight tributes to purity of purpose.

Forster had that genuine sympathy with men of letters which entitled him to be their biographer, and all his works in that department have a special charm, habitually gained only by a subtle and earnest intellect.

It is a singular coincidence that the writers of two of the most brilliant records of travel of their time should have been law students in Barry Cornwall's office. Kinglake, the author of "Eothen," and Warburton, the author of "The Crescent and the Cross," were at one period both engaged as pupils in their profession under the guidance of Mr. Procter. He frequently spoke with pride of his two law students, and when Warburton perished at sea, his grief for his brilliant friend was deep and abiding. Kinglake's later literary fame was always a pleasure to the historian's old master, and no one in England loved better to point out the fine passages in the "History of the Invasion of the Crimea" than the old poet in Weymouth Street.

"Blackwood" and the "Quarterly Review" railed at Procter and his author friends for a long period; but how true is the saying of Macaulay, "that the place of books in the public estimation is fixed, not by what is written *about* them, but by

HAZLITT.

what is written in them!" No man was more decried in his day than Procter's friend, William Hazlitt. The poet had for the critic a genuine admiration; and I have heard him dilate with a kind of rapture over the critic's fine sayings, quoting abundant passages from the essays. Procter would never hear any disparagement of his friend's ability and keenness. I recall his earnest but restrained indignation one day, when some person compared Hazlitt with a diffusive modern writer of notes on the theatre, and I remember with what contempt, in his sweet forgivable way, the old man spoke of much that passes nowadays for criticism. He said Hazlitt was exactly the opposite of Lord Chesterfield, who advised his son, if he could not get at a thing in a straight line to try the serpentine one. There were no crooked pathways in Hazlitt's intellect. His style is brilliant, but never cloyed with ornamentation. Hazlitt's paper on Gifford was thought by Procter to be as pungent a bit of writing as had appeared in his day, and he quoted this paragraph as a sample of its biting justice: "Mr. Gifford is admirably qualified for the situation he has held for many years as editor of the 'Quarterly' by a happy combination of defects, natural and acquired." In one of his letters to me Procter writes, "I despair of the age that has forgotten to read Hazlitt."

Procter was a delightful prose writer, as well as

a charming poet. Having met in old magazines and annuals several of his essays and stories, and admiring their style and spirit, I induced him, after much persuasion, to collect and publish in America his prose works. The result was a couple of volumes, which were brought out in Boston in 1853. In them there are perhaps no "thoughts that wander through eternity," but they abound in fancies which the reader will recognize as agile

"Daughters of the earth and sun."

In them there is nothing loud or painful, and whoever really loves "a good book," and knows it to be such on trial, will find Barry Cornwall's "Essays and Tales in Prose" most delectable reading. "Imparadised," as Milton hath the word, on a summer hillside, or tented by the cool salt wave, no better afternoon literature can be selected. One will never meet with distorted metaphor or tawdry rhetoric in Barry's thoughtful pages, but will find a calm philosophy and a beautiful faith, very precious and profitable in these days of doubt and insecurity of intellect. There is a respite and a sympathy in this fine spirit, and so I commend him heartily in times so full of turmoil and suspicion as these. One of the stories in the first volume of these prose writings, called "The Man-Hunter," is quite equal in power to any of the graphic pieces of a similar character ever written by De Quincey or Dickens,

OLD ACQUAINTANCE. 97

but the tone in these books is commonly more tender and inclining to melancholy. What, for instance, could be more heart-moving than these passages of his on the death of little children?

"I scarcely know how it is, but the deaths of children seem to me always less premature than those of elder persons. Not that they are in fact so; but it is because they themselves have little or no relation to time or maturity. Life seems a race which they have yet to run entirely. They have made no progress toward the goal. They are born — nothing further. But it seems hard, when a man has toiled high up the steep hill of knowledge, that he should be cast like Sisyphus, downward in a moment; that he who has worn the day and wasted the night in gathering the gold of science should be, with all his wealth of learning, all his accumulations, made bankrupt at once. What becomes of all the riches of the soul, the piles and pyramids of precious thoughts which men heap together? Where are Shakespeare's imagination, Bacon's learning, Galileo's dream? Where is the sweet fancy of Sidney, the airy spirit of Fletcher, and Milton's thought severe? Methinks such things should not die and dissipate, when a hair can live for centuries, and a brick of Egypt will last three thousand years! I am content to believe that the mind of man survives (somewhere or other) his clay.

"I was once present at the death of a little child. I will not pain the reader by portraying its agonies; but when its breath was gone, its *life*, (nothing more than a cloud of smoke!) and it lay like a waxen image before me, I turned my eyes to its moaning mother, and sighed out my few words of comfort. But I am a beggar in grief. I can feel and sigh and look kindly, I think; but I have nothing to give. My tongue deserts me. I know the inutility of too soon comforting. I know that *I* should weep were I the loser, and I let the tears have their way. Sometimes a word or two I can muster: a 'Sigh no more!' and 'Dear lady, do not grieve!' but further I am mute and useless."

I have many letters and kind little notes which Procter used to write me during the years I knew him best. His tricksy fancies peeped out in his correspondence, and several of his old friends in England thought no literary man of his time had a better epistolary style. His neat and elegant chirography on the back of a letter was always a delightful foretaste of something good inside, and I never received one of his welcome missives that did not contain, no matter how brief it happened to be, welcome passages of wit or affectionate interest.

In one of his early letters to me he says:—

"There is no one rising hereabouts in literature. I suppose our national genius is taking a mechanical turn. And, in truth, it is much better to make a good steam-engine than to manufacture a bad poem. 'Building the lofty rhyme' is a good thing, but our present buildings are of a low order, and seldom reach the Attic. This piece of wit will scarcely throw you into a fit, I imagine, your risible muscles being doubtless kept in good order."

In another he writes:—

"I see you have some capital names in the 'Atlantic Monthly.' If they will only put forth their strength, there is no doubt as to the result, but the misfortune is that persons who write anonymously *don't* put forth their strength, in general. I was a magazine writer for no less than a dozen years, and I felt that no personal credit or responsibility attached to my literary trifling, and although I sometimes did pretty well (for me), yet I never did my best."

As I read over again the portfolio of his letters to me, bearing date from 1848 to 1866, I find many passages of interest, but most of them are too personal for type. A few extracts, however, I cannot resist copying. Some of his epistles are enriched with a song or a sonnet, then just written, and there are also frequent references in them to American editions of his poetical and prose works, which he collected at the request of his Boston publishers.

In June, 1851, he writes: —

"I have encountered a good many of your countrymen here lately, but have been introduced only to a few. I found Mr. Norton, who has returned to you, and Mr. Dwight, who is still here, I believe, very intelligent and agreeable.

"If all Americans were like them and yourself, and if all Englishmen were like Kenyon and (so far as regards a desire to judge fairly) myself, I think there would be little or no quarrelling between our small island and your great continent.

"Our glass palace is a perpetual theme for small-talk. It usurps the place of the weather, which is turned adrift, or laid up in ordinary for future use. Nevertheless it (I mean the palace) is a remarkable achievement, after all; and I speak sincerely when I say, 'All honor and glory to Paxton!' If the strings of my poor little lyre were not rusty and overworn, I think I should try to sing some of my nonsense verses before his image, and add to the idolatry already existing.

"If you have hotter weather in America than that which is at present burning and blistering us here, you are entitled to pity. If it continue much longer, I shall be held in solution for the remainder of my days, and shall be remark-

able as 'Oxygen, the poet' (reduced to his natural weakness and simplicity by the hot summer of 1851), instead of
"Your very sincere and obliged
"B. W. PROCTER."

Here is a brief reference to Judd's remarkable novel, forming part of a note written to me in 1852: —

"Thanks for 'Margaret' (the book, *not* the woman), that you have sent me. When will you want it back? and who is the author? There is a great deal of clever writing in it, — great observation of nature, and also of **character** among a certain class of persons. But it is almost too minute, and for *me* decidedly too theological. You see what irreligious people we are here. I shall come over to one of your camp-meetings and *try* to be converted. What will they administer in such a case? brimstone or brandy? I shall try the latter first."

Here is a letter bearing date "Thursday night, November 25, 1852," in which he refers to his own writings, and copies a charming song : —

"Your letter, announcing the arrival of the little preface, reached me last night. I shall look out for the book in about three weeks hence, as you tell me that they are all printed. You Americans are a **rapid race.** When I thought you were in Scotland, lo, you had touched the soil of Boston; and when I thought you were unpacking my poor MS., tumbling it out of your great trunk, behold! it is arranged — it is in the printer's hands — it is *printed* — published — it is — ah! would I could add, SOLD! That, after all, is the grand triumph in Boston as well as London.

"Well, since it is not sold yet, let us be generous and give a few copies away. Indeed, such is my weakness, that I would sometimes rather give than sell. In the present instance you will do me the kindness to send a copy each to Mr. Charles Sumner, Mr. Hillard, Mr. Norton: but no — my wife requests to be the donor to Mr. Norton, so you must, if you please, write his name in the first leaf and state that it comes from '*Mrs.* Procter.' I liked him very much when I met him in London, and I should wish him to be reminded of his English acquaintance.

"I am writing to you at eleven o'clock at night, after a long and busy day, and I write *now* rather than wait for a little inspiration, because the mail, I believe, starts to-morrow. The unwilling Minerva is at my elbow, and I feel that every sentence I write, were it pounded ten times in a mortar, would come out again unleavened and heavy. Braying some people in a mortar, you know, is but a weary and unprofitable process.

"You speak of London as a delightful place. I don't know how it may be in the white-bait season, but at present it is foggy, rainy, cold, dull. Half of us are unwell and the other half dissatisfied. Some are apprehensive of an invasion, — not an impossible event; some writing odes to the Duke of Wellington; and I am putting my good friend to sleep with the flattest prose that ever dropped from an English pen. I wish that it were better; I wish that it were even worse; but it is the most undeniable twaddle. I must go to bed, and invoke the Muses in the morning. At present, I cannot touch one of their petticoats.

"A SLEEPY SONG.

"Sing! sing me to sleep!
    With gentle words, in some sweet slumberous measure,
Such as lone poet on some shady steep
    Sings to the silence in his noonday leisure.

"Sing! as the river sings,
    When gently it flows between soft banks of flowers,
And the bee murmurs, and the cuckoo brings
    His faint May music, 'tween the golden showers.

"Sing! O divinest tone!
  I sink beneath some wizard's charming wand;
I yield, I move, by soothing breezes blown,
  O'er twilight shores, into the Dreaming Land!

"I read the above to you when you were in London. It will appear in an Annual edited by Miss Power (Lady Blessington's niece).

"*Friday Morning.*

"The wind blowing down the chimney; the rain sprinkling my windows. The English Apollo hides his head — you can scarcely see him on the 'misty mountain-tops' (those brick ones which you remember in Portland Place).

"My friend Thackeray is gone to America, and I hope is, by this time, in the United States. He goes to New York, and afterward I *suppose* (but I don't know) to Boston and Philadelphia. Have you seen *Esmond?* There are parts of it charmingly written. His pathos is to me very touching. I believe that the best mode of making one's way to a person's head is — through his heart.

"I hope that your literary men will like some of my little prose matters. I know that they will *try* to like them; but the papers have been written so long, and all, or almost all, written so hastily, that I have my misgivings. However, they must take their chance.

"Had I leisure to complete something that I began two or three years ago, and in which I have written a chapter or two, I should reckon more surely on success; but I shall probably never finish the thing, although I contemplated only one volume.

"(If you cannot read this letter apply to the printer's devil. — Hibernicus.)

"Farewell. All good be with you. My wife desires to be kindly remembered by you.

"Always yours, very sincerely,

"B. W. PROCTER.

"P. S. — Can you contrive to send Mr. Willis a copy of the prose book? If so, pray do."

In February, 1853, he writes: —

"Those famous volumes, the advent of which was some time since announced by the great transatlantic trumpet, have duly arrived. My wife is properly grateful for her copy, which, indeed, impresses both of us with respect for the American skill in binding. Neither too gay to be gaudy, nor too grave, so as to affect the theological, it hits that happy medium which agrees with the tastes of most people and disgusts none. We should flatter ourselves that it is intended to represent the matter within, but that we are afraid of incurring the sin of vanity, and the indiscretion of taking appearances too much upon trust. We suspend our conjectures on this very interesting subject. The whole getting up of the book is excellent.

"For the little scraps of (critical) sugar enclosed in your letter, due thanks. These will sweeten our imagination for some time to come.

"I have been obliged to give all the copies you sent me away. I dare say you will not grudge me four or five copies more, to be sent at your convenience, of course. Let me hear from you at the same time. You can give me one of those frequent quarters of an hour which I know you now devote to a meditation on 'things in general.'

"I am glad that you like Thackeray. He is well worth your liking. I trust to his making both friends and money in America, and to his *keeping* both. I am not so sure of the money, however, for he has a liberal hand. I should have liked to have been at one of the dinners you speak of. (When shall you begin that *bridge?* You seem to be a long time about it. It will, I dare say, be a bridge of boats, after all.) . . . .

"I was reading (rather re-reading) the other evening the introductory chapter to the ' Scarlet Letter.' It is admirably written. Not having any great sympathy with a custom-house, — nor, indeed, with Salem, except that it seems to be Hawthorne's birthplace, — all my attention was concentrated on the *style*, which seems to me excellent.

"The most striking book which has been recently published here is 'Villette,' by the authoress of 'Jane Eyre,' who, as you know, is a Miss Brontë. The book does not give one the most pleasing notion of the authoress, perhaps, but it is very clever, graphic, vigorous. It is 'man's meat,' and not the whipped syllabub, which is *all* froth, without any jam at the bottom. The scene of the drama is Brussels.

"I was sorry to hear of poor Willis. Our critics here were too severe upon him. . . . .

"The Frost King (vulg. Jack Frost) has come down upon us with all his might. Banished from the pleasant shores of Boston, he has come with his cold scythe and ice pincers to our undefended little island, and is tyrannizing in every corner and over every part of every person. Nothing is too great for him, nothing too mean. He condescends even to lay hold of the nose (an offence for which any one below the dignity of a King — or a President — would be kicked). As for me, I have taken refuge in

"A SONG, WITH A MORAL.

"When the winter bloweth loud,
  And the earth is in a shroud,
  Frozen rain or sleety snow
  Dimming every dream below, —
    There is e'er a spot of green
    Whence the heavens may be seen.

"When our purse is shrinking fast,
  And our friend is lost, (the last!)
  And the world doth pour its pain,
  Sharper than the frozen rain, —
    There is still a spot of green
    Whence the heavens may be seen.

"Let us never meet despair
  While the little spot is there;

> Winter brighteneth into May,
> And sullen night to sunny day, —
>   Seek we then the spot of green
>   Whence the heavens may be seen.

"I have left myself little space for more small-talk. I must, therefore, conclude with wishing that your English dreams may continue bright, and that when they begin to fade you will come and *relume* at one of the white-bait dinners of which you used to talk in such terms of rapture.

"Have I space to say that I am very truly yours?

"B. W. PROCTER."

A few months later, in the same year (1853), he sits by his open window in London, on a morning of spring, and sends off the following pleasant words : —

"You also must now be in the first burst and sunshine of spring. Your spear-grass is showing its points, your succulent grass its richness, even your little plant [?] (so useful for certain invalids) is seen here and there; primroses are peeping out in your neighborhood, and you are looking for cowslips to come. I say nothing of your hawthorns (from the common May to the classic Nathaniel), except that I trust they are thriving, and like to put forth a world of blossoms soon.

> 'With all this wealth, present and future,
>   The yellow cowslip and the pale primrose,'

you will doubtless feel disposed to scatter your small coins abroad on the poor, and, among other things, to forward to your humble correspondent those copies of B—— C——'s prose works which you promised I know not how long ago. 'He who gives *speedily*,' they say, 'gives twice.' I quote, as you see, from the Latins.

"I have just got the two additional volumes of De Quincey, for which — thanks! I have not seen Mr. Parker, who brought them, and who left his card here yesterday, but I have asked if he will come and breakfast with me on Sunday, — my only certain leisure day. Your De Quincey is a man of a good deal of reading, and has thought on divers and sundry matters; but he is evidently so thoroughly well pleased with the Sieur 'Thomas De Quincey' that his self-sufficiency spoils even his best works. Then some of his facts are, I hear, *quasi* facts only, not unfrequently. He has his moments when he sleeps, and becomes oblivious of all but the aforesaid 'Thomas,' who pervades both his sleeping and waking visions. I, like all authors, am glad to have a little praise now and then (it is my hydromel), but it must be dispensed by others. I do not think it decent to manufacture the sweet liquor myself, and I hate a coxcomb, whether in dress or print.

"We have little or no literary news here. Our poets are all going to the poorhouse (except Tennyson), and our prose writers are piling up their works for the next 5th of November, when there will be a great bonfire. It is deuced lucky that my immortal (ah! I am De Quinceying) — I mean my humble — performances were printed in America, so that they will escape. By the by, are they on foolscap? for I forgot to caution you on that head.

"I have been spending a week at Liverpool, where I rejoiced to hear that Hawthorne's appointment was settled, and that it was a valuable post; but I hear that it lasts for three years only. This is melancholy. I hope, however, that he will 'realize' (as you transatlantics say) as much as he can during his consulate, and that your next President will have the good taste and the good sense to renew his lease for three years more.

"I have not seen Mrs. Stowe. I shall probably meet her somewhere or other when she comes to London.

"I dare not ask after Mr. Longfellow. He was kind enough to write me a very agreeable letter some time ago, which I ought to have answered. I dare say that he has forgotten it, but my conscience is a serpent that gives me a bite or a sting every now and then when I think of him. The first time I am in fit condition (I mean in point of brightness) to reply to so famous a correspondent, I shall try what an English pen and ink will enable me to say. In the mean time, God be thanked for all things!

"My wife heard from Thackeray about ten days ago. He speaks gratefully of the kindness that he has met with in America. Among other things, it appears that he has seen something of your slaves, whom he represents as leading a very easy life, and as being fat, cheerful, and happy. Nevertheless, *I* (for one) would rather be a free man, — such is the singularity of my opinions. If my prosings should ever in the course of the next twenty years require to be reprinted, pray take note of the above opinion.

"And now I have no more paper; I have scarcely room left to say that I hope you are well, and to remind you that for your ten lines of writing I have sent you back a hundred. Give my best compliments to all whom I know, personally or otherwise. God be with you!

"Yours, very sincerely,

"B. W. PROCTER."

Procter always seemed to be astounded at the travelling spirit of Americans, and in his letters he makes frequent reference to our "national propensity," as he calls it.

"Half an hour ago," he writes in July, 1853, "we had three of your countrymen here to lunch, — countrymen, I mean, Hibernically, for two of them wore petticoats. They are all going to Switzerland, France, Italy, Egypt, and Syria. What an adventurous race you are, you Americans! Here the women go merely 'from the blue bed to the brown,' and think that they have travelled and seen the world. I myself should not care much to be confined to a circle reaching six or seven miles round London. There are the fresh winds and wild thyme on Hampstead Heath, and from Richmond you may survey the Naiades. Highgate, where Coleridge lived, Enfield, where Charles Lamb dwelt, are not far off. Turning eastward, there is the river Lea, in which Izaak Walton fished; and farther on — ha! what do I see? What are those little fish frisking in the batter (the great Naval Hospital close by), which fixed the affections of the enamored American while he resided in London, and have been floating in his dreams ever since? They are said by the naturalists to be of the species *Blandamentum album*, and are by vulgar aldermen spoken carelessly of as *whitebait*.

"London is full of carriages, full of strangers, full of parties feasting on strawberries and ices and other things intended to allay the heat of summer; but the Summer herself (fickle virgin) keeps back, or has been stopped somewhere or other, — perhaps at the Liverpool custom-house, where the very brains of men (their books) are held in durance, as I know to my cost.

"Thackeray is about to publish a new work in numbers, — a serial, as the newspapers call it. Thomas Carlyle is publishing (a sixpenny matter) in favor of the slave-trade. Novelists of all shades are plying their trades. Husbands are killing their wives in every day's newspaper. Burglars are peaching against each other; there is no longer honor among thieves. I am starting for Leicester on a week's expedition amidst the mad people; and the Emperor of Russia has crossed the Pruth, and intends to make a tour of Turkey.

"All this appears to me little better than idle, restless vanity. O my friend, what a fuss and a pother we are all making, we little flies who are going round on the great wheel of time! To-day we are flickering and buzzing about, our little bits of wings glittering in the sunshine, and tomorrow we are safe enough in the little crevice at the back of the fireplace, or hid in the folds of the old curtain, shut up, stiff and torpid, for the long winter. What do you say to that profound reflection?

"I struggle against the lassitude which besets me, and strive in vain to be either sensible or jocose. I had better say farewell."

On Christmas day, 1854, he writes in rather flagging spirits, induced by ill health: —

"I have owed you a letter for these many months, my good friend. I am afraid to think *how* long, lest the interest on the debt should have exceeded the capital, and be beyond my power to pay.

"You must be good-natured and excuse me, for I have been ill — very frequently — and dispirited. A bodily complaint torments me, that has tormented me for the last two years. I no longer look at the world through a rose-colored glass. The prospect, I am sorry to say, is gray, grim, dull, barren, full of withered leaves, without flowers, or if there be any, all of them trampled down, soiled, discolored, and without fragrance. You see what a bit of half-smoked glass I am looking through. At all events, you must see how entirely I am disabled from returning, except in sober sentences, the lively and good-natured letters and other things which you have sent me from America. They were welcome, and I thank you for them now, in a few words, as you observe, but sincerely. I am somewhat brief, even in my gratitude. Had I been in braver spirits, I might have spurred my poor Pegasus, and sent you some lines on the Alma, or the Inkerman, — bloody battles, but exhibiting marks not to be mistaken of the old English heroism, which, after all is said about the enervating effects of luxury, is as grand and manifest as in the ancient fights which English history talks of so much. Even you, sternest of republicans, will, I think, be proud of the indomitable courage of Englishmen, and gladly refer to your old paternity. I, at least, should be proud of Americans fighting after the same fashion (and without doubt they *would* fight thus), just as old people exult in the brave conduct of their runaway sons. I cannot read of these later battles without the tears coming into my eyes. It is said by 'our correspondent' at New York that the folks there rejoice in the losses and disasters of the allies. This can never be the case, surely? No one whose opinion is worth a rap can rejoice at any success of the Czar, whose double-dealing and unscrupulous greediness must have rendered him an object of loathing to every well-thinking man. But what have I to do with politics, or you? Our 'pleasant object and serene employ' are books, books. Let us return to pacific thoughts.

"What a number of things have happened since I saw you! I looked for you in the last spring, little dreaming that so fat and flourishing a 'Statesman' could be overthrown by a little fever. I had even begun some doggerel, announcing to you the advent of the white-bait, which I imagined were likely to be all eaten up in your absence. My memory is so bad that I cannot recollect half a dozen lines, probably not one, as it originally stood.

"I was at Liverpool last June. After two or three attempts I contrived to seize on the famous Nathaniel Hawthorne. Need I say that I like him *very* much? He is very sensible, very genial,—a little shy, I think (for an American!)—and altogether extremely agreeable. I wish that I could see more of him, but our orbits are wide apart. Now and then—once in two years—I diverge into and cross his circle, but at other times we are separated by a space amounting to 210 miles. He has three children, and a nice little wife, who has good-humor engraved on her countenance.

"As to verse—yes, I have begun a dozen trifling things, which are in my drawer unfinished; poor rags with ink upon them, none of them, I am afraid, properly labelled for posterity. I was for six weeks at Ryde, in the Isle of Wight, this year, but so unwell that I could not write a line, scarcely read one; sitting out in the sun, eating, drinking, sleeping, and sometimes (poor soul!) imagining I was thinking. One Sunday I saw a magnificent steamer go by, and on placing my eye to the telescope I saw some Stars and Stripes (streaming from the mast-head) that carried me away to Boston. By the way, when *will* you finish the bridge?

"I hear strange hints of you all quarrelling about the slave question. Is it so? You are so happy and prosperous in America that you must be on the lookout for clouds, surely! When you see Emerson, Longfellow, Sumner, any one I know, pray bespeak for me a kind thought or word from them."

Procter was always on the lookout for Hawthorne, whom he greatly admired. In November, 1855, he says, in a brief letter: —

"I have not seen Hawthorne since I wrote to you. He came to London this summer, but, I am sorry to say, did not inquire for me. As it turned out, I was absent from town, but sent him (by Mrs. Russell Sturgis) a letter of introduction to Leigh Hunt, who was very much pleased with him. Poor Hunt! he is the most genial of men; and, now that his wife is confined to her bed by rheumatism, is recovering himself, and, I hope, doing well. He asked to come and see me the other day. I willingly assented, and when I saw him — grown old and sad and broken down in health — all my ancient liking for him revived.

"You ask me to send you some verse. I accordingly send you a scrap of recent manufacture, and you will observe that instead of forwarding my epic on Sevastopol, I select something that is fitter for these present vernal love days than the bluster of heroic verse: —

"SONG.

"Within the chambers of her breast
Love lives and makes his spicy nest,

Midst downy blooms and fragrant flowers,
And there he dreams away the hours —
  There let him rest!
Some time hence, when the cuckoo sings,
I'll come by night and bind his wings, —
Bind him that he shall not roam
From his warm white virgin home.

"Maiden of the summer season,
  Angel of the rosy time,
Come, unless some graver reason
  Bid thee scorn my rhyme;
Come from thy serener height,
On a golden cloud descending,
Come ere Love hath taken flight,
And let thy stay be like the light,
When its glory hath no ending
  In the Northern night!"

Now and then we get a glimpse of Thackeray in his letters. In one of them he says: —

"Thackeray came a few days ago and read one of his lectures at our house (that on George the Third), and we asked about a dozen persons to come and hear it, among the rest, your handsome countrywoman, Mrs. R—— S——. It was very pleasant, with that agreeable intermixture of tragedy and comedy that tells so well when judiciously managed. He will not print them for some time to come, intending to read them at some of the principal places in England, and perhaps Scotland.

"What are you doing in America? You are too happy and independent! 'O fortunatos Agricolas, sua si bona nôrint!' I am not quite sure of my Latin (which is rusty from old age), but I am sure of the sentiment, which is that when people are too happy, they don't know it, and so take to quarrelling to relieve the monotony of their blue sky.

Some of these days you will split your great kingdom in two, I suppose, and then —

"My wife's mother, Mrs. Basil Montagu, is very ill, and we are apprehensive of a fatal result, which, in truth, the mere fact of her age (eighty-two or eighty-three) is enough to warrant. Ah, this terrible *age!* The young people, I dare say, think that we live too long. Yet how short it is to look back on life! Why, I saw the house the other day where I used to play with a wooden sword when I was five years old! It cannot surely be eighty years ago! What has occurred since? Why, nothing that is worth putting down on paper. A few nonsense verses, a flogging or two (richly deserved), and a few white-bait dinners, and the whole is reckoned up. Let us begin again." [Here he makes some big letters in a school-boy hand, which have a very pathetic look on the page.]

In a letter written in 1856 he gives me a graphic picture of sad times in India : —

"All our anxiety here at present is the Indian mutiny. We ourselves have great cause for trouble. Our son (the only son I have, indeed) escaped from Delhi lately. He is now at Meerut. He and four or five other officers, four women, and a child escaped. The men were obliged to drop the women a fearful height from the walls of the fort, amidst showers of bullets. A round shot passed within a yard of my son, and one of the ladies had a bullet through her shoulder. They were seven days and seven nights in the jungle, without money or meat, scarcely any clothes, no shoes. They forded rivers, lay on the wet ground at night, lapped water from the puddles, and finally reached Meerut. The lady (the mother of the three other ladies) had not her wound dressed, or seen, indeed, for upward of a week. Their feet were full of thorns. My son had nothing but a shirt, a pair of trousers, and a flannel waistcoat. How they contrived to *live* I don't know; I suppose from small gifts of rice, etc., from the natives.

"When I find any little thing now that disturbs my serenity, and which I might in former times have magnified into an evil, I think of what Europeans suffer from the vengeance of the Indians, and pass it by in quiet.

"I received Mr. Hillard's epitaph on my dear kind friend Kenyon. Thank him in my name for it. There are some copies to be reserved of a lithograph now in progress (a portrait of Kenyon) for his American friends. Should it be completed in time, Mr. Sumner will be asked to take them over. I have put down your name for one of those who would wish to have this little memento of a good kind man. . . . .

"I shall never visit America, be assured, or the continent of Europe, or any distant region. I have reached nearly to the length of my tether. I have grown old and apathetic and stupid. All I care for, in the way of personal enjoyment, is quiet, ease, — to have nothing to do, nothing to think of. My only glance is backward. There is so little before me that I would rather not look that way."

In a later letter he again speaks of his son and the war in India: —

"My son is *not* in the list of killed and wounded, thank God! He was before Delhi, having volunteered thither after his escape. We trust that he is at present safe, but every mail is pregnant with bloody tidings, and we do not find ourselves yet in a position to rejoice securely. What a terrible war this Indian war is! Are all people of black blood cruel, cowardly, and treacherous? If it were a case of great oppression on our part, I could understand and (almost) excuse it; but it is from the *spoiled* portion of the Hindostanees that the revengeful mutiny has arisen. One thing is quite clear, that whatever luxury and refinement have done for our race (for I include Americans with English), they have not diminished the courage and endurance and heroism for which I think we have formerly been famous. We are the same Saxons still. There has never been fiercer fighting than in some of the battles that have lately taken place in India. When I look back on the old history books, and see that *all* history consists of little else than the bloody feuds of nation with nation, I almost wonder that God has not extinguished the cruel, selfish animals that we dignify with the name of men. No — I cry forgiveness: let the women live, if they can, without the men. I used the word 'men' only."

Here is a pleasant paragraph about "Aurora Leigh": —

"The most successful book of the season has been Mrs. Browning's 'Aurora Leigh.' I could wish some things altered, I confess; but as it is, it is by far (a hundred times over) the finest poem ever written by a woman. We know little or nothing of Sappho, — nothing to induce comparison, — and all other wearers of petticoats must courtesy to the ground."

In several of his last letters to me there are frequent allusions to our civil war. Here is an extract from an epistle written in 1861: —

"We read with painful attention the accounts of your great quarrel in America. We know nothing beyond what we are told by the New York papers, and these are the stories of *one* of the combatants. I am afraid that, however you may mend the schism, you will never be so strong again. I hope, however, that something may arise to terminate the bloodshed; for, after all, fighting is an unsatisfactory way of coming at the truth. If you were to stand up at once (and finally) against the slave-trade, your band of soldiers would have a more decided *principle* to fight for. But —

"— But I really know little or nothing. I hope that at Boston you are comparatively peaceful, and I know that you are more abolitionist than in the more southern countries.

"There is nothing new doing here in the way of books.

The last book I have seen is called 'Tannhäuser,' published by Chapman and Hall,—a poem under feigned names, but *really* written by Robert Lytton and Julian Fane. It is not good enough for the first, but (as I conjecture) too good for the last. The songs which decide the contest of the bards are the worst portions of the book.

"I read some time ago a novel which has not made much noise, but which is prodigiously clever,—'City and Suburb.' The story hangs in parts, but it is full of weighty sentences. We have no poet *since* Tennyson except Robert Lytton, who, you know, calls himself Owen Meredith. Poetry in England is assuming a new character, and not a better character. It has a sort of pre-Raphaelite tendency which does not suit my aged feelings. I am for Love, or the World well lost. But I forget that, if I live beyond the 21st of next November, I shall be *seventy-four* years of age. I have been obliged to resign my Commissionership of Lunacy, not being able to bear the pain of travelling. By this I lose about £900 a year. I am, therefore, sufficiently poor even for a poet. Browning, as you know, has lost his wife. He is coming with his little boy to live in England. I rejoice at this, for I think that the English should live in England, especially in their youth, when people learn things that they never forget afterward."

Near the close of 1864 he writes:—

"Since I last heard from you, nothing except what is melancholy seems to have taken place. You seem all busy killing each other in America. Some friends of yours and several friends of mine have died. Among the last I cannot help placing Nathaniel Hawthorne, for whom I had a sincere regard. .... He was about your best prose writer, I think, and intermingled with his humor was a great deal of tenderness. To die so soon!

"You are so easily affronted in America, if we (English) say anything about putting an end to your war, that I will not venture to hint at the subject. Nevertheless, I wish that you were all at peace again, for your own sakes and for the sake of human nature. I detest fighting now, although I was a great admirer of fighting in my youth. My youth? I wonder where it has gone. It has left me with gray hairs and rheumatism, and plenty of (too many other) infirmities. I stagger and stumble along, with almost seventy-six years on my head, upon failing limbs, which no longer enable me to walk half a mile. I see a great deal, all behind me (the Past), but the prospect before me is not cheerful. Sometimes I wish that I had tried harder for what is called Fame, but generally (as now) I care very little about it. After all, — unless one could be Shakespeare, which (clearly) is not an easy matter, — of what value is a little puff of smoke from a review? If we could settle permanently who is to be the Homer or Shakespeare of our time, it might be worth something; but we cannot. Is it Jones, or Smith, or ——? Alas! I get short-sighted on this point, and cannot penetrate the impenetrable dark. Make my remembrances acceptable to Longfellow, to Lowell, to Emerson, and to any one else who remembers me.

"Yours, ever sincerely,

"B. W. Procter."

And here are a few paragraphs from the last letter I ever received from Procter's loving hand: —

"Although I date this from Weymouth Street, yet I am writing 140 or 150 miles away from London. Perhaps this temporary retreat from our great, noisy, turbulent city reminds me that I have been very unmindful of your letter, received long ago. But I have been busy, and my writing now is not a simple matter, as it was fifty years ago. I have great difficulty in forming the letters, and you would be surprised to learn with what labor *this* task is performed. Then I have been incessantly occupied in writing (I refer to the *mechanical* part only) the 'Memoir of Charles Lamb.' It is not my book, — i. e. not my property, — but one which I was hired to write, and it forms my last earnings. You will have heard of the book (perhaps seen it) some time since. It has been very well received. I would not have engaged myself on anything else, but I had great regard for Charles Lamb, and so (somehow or other) I have contrived to reach the end.

"I *have* already (long ago) written something about Hazlitt, but I have received more than one application for it, in case I can manage to complete my essay. As in the case of Lamb, I am really the only person living who knew much about his daily life. I have not, however, quite the same incentive to carry me on. Indeed, I am not certain that I should be able to travel to the real Finis.

"My wife is very grateful for the copies of my dear Adelaide's poems which you sent her. She appears surprised to hear that I have not transmitted her thanks to you before.

"We get the 'Atlantic Monthly' regularly. I need not tell you how much better the poetry is than at its commencement. Very good is 'Released,' in the July number, and several of the stories; but they are in London, and I cannot particularize them.

"We were very much pleased with Colonel Holmes, the son of your friend and contributor. He seems a very intelligent, modest young man; as little military as need be, and, like Coriolanus, not baring his wounds (if he has any) for public gaze. When you see Dr. Holmes, pray tell him how much I and my wife liked his son.

"We are at the present moment rusticating at Malvern Wells. We are on the side of a great hill (which you would call small in America), and our intercourse is only with the flowers and bees and swallows of the season. Sometimes we encounter a wasp, which I suppose comes from over seas!

"The Storys are living two or three miles off, and called upon us a few days ago. You have not seen *his* Sibyl, which I think very fine, and as containing a *very great* future. But the young poets generally disappoint us, and are too content with startling us into admiration of their first works, and then go to sleep.

"I wish that I had, when younger, made more notes about my contemporaries; for, being of no faction in politics, it happens that I have known far more literary men than any other person of my time. In counting up the names of persons known to me who were, in some way or other, *connected* with literature, I reckoned up more than one hundred. But then I have had more than sixty years to do this in. My first acquaintance of this sort was Bowles, the poet. This was about 1805.

"Although I can scarcely write, I am able to say, in conclusion, that I am

"Very sincerely yours,

"B. W. PROCTER."

Procter was an ardent student of the works of our older English dramatists, and he had a special fondness for such writers as Decker, Marlowe, Heywood, Webster, and Fletcher. Many of his own dramatic scenes are modelled on that passionate and romantic school. He had great relish for a good modern novel, too; and I recall the titles of several which he recommended warmly for my perusal and republication in America. When I first came to know him, the duties of his office as a Commissioner obliged him to travel about the kingdom, sometimes on long journeys, and he told me his pocket companion was a cheap reprint of Emerson's "Essays," which he found such agreeable reading that he never left home without it. Longfellow's "Hyperion" was another of his favorite books during the years he was on duty.

Among the last agreeable visits I made to the old poet was one with reference to a proposition of his own to omit several songs and other short poems from a new issue of his works then in press. I stoutly opposed the ignoring of certain old favorites of mine, and the poet's wife joined with me in deciding against the author in his proposal to cast aside so many beautiful songs, — songs as well worth saving as any in the volume. Procter argued that, being past seventy, he had now reached to years of discretion, and that his judgment ought to be followed without a murmur. I held out firm to the end of our discussion, and we settled the matter with this compromise : he was to expunge whatever he chose from the English edition, but I was to have my own way with the American one. So to this day the American reprint is the only complete collection of Barry Cornwall's earliest pieces, for I held on to all the old lyrics, without discarding a single line.

The poet's figure was short and full, and his voice had a low, veiled tone habitually in it, which made it sometimes difficult to hear distinctly what he was saying. When in conversation, he liked to be very near his listener, and thus stand, as it were, on confidential ground with him. His turn of thought was cheerful among his friends, and he proceeded readily into a vein of wit and nimble expression. Verbal felicity seemed natural to him, and his epithets, evidently unprepared, were always perfect. He disliked cant and hard ways of judging character. He praised easily. He had no wish to stand in anybody's shoes but his own, and he said, "There is no literary vice of a darker shade than envy." Talleyrand's recipe for perfect happiness was the opposite to his. He impressed every one who came near him as a born gentleman, chivalrous and generous in a marked degree, and it was the habit of those who knew him to have an affection for him. Altering a line of Pope, this counsel might have been safely tendered to all the authors of his day, —

"Disdain whatever *Procter's mind* disdains."

www.ingramcontent.com/pod-product-compliance
Lightning Source LLC
Chambersburg PA
CBHW021942160426
43195CB00011B/1192